HOTEL/RESTAURANT MANAGEMENT
CAREER STARTER

HOTEL/RESTAURANT MANAGEMENT

career starter

Lauren Starkey

New York

Library of Congress Cataloging-in-Publication Data:
Starkey, Lauren B., 1962–
    Hotel/restaurant management career starter / Lauren B. Starkey.—1st ed.
      p. cm.
  ISBN 1-57685-411-6
  1. Hotel management. 2. Restaurant management. I. Title.
    TX911.3.M27 S6985 2002
    647.94'068—dc21

                                2002001383

Printed in the United States of America
9 8 7 6 5 4 3 2 1
First Edition

ISBN 1-57685-411-6

For more information or to place an order, contact LearningExpress at:
  900 Broadway
  Suite 604
  New York, NY 10003

Or visit us at:
  www.learnatest.com

About the Author

Lauren Starkey is a writer and editor, specializing in educational and reference works, with over ten years of experience. For eight years, she worked on the Oxford English Dictionary. She lives in Essex, Vermont, with her husband, Gorden, and children, Emma, Graham, and Cameron.

Contents

Contents

Introduction

Why Become a Hotel or Restaurant Manager?

HOTEL AND restaurant managers work in the hospitality industry, providing services to millions of people around the world every day. Most people are familiar with the setting in which these managers work, having enjoyed meals in restaurants and stayed in hotels. But how many know what goes on behind the scenes? Depending on the size of the establishment, there may be hundreds of people involved in the process of providing a hotel room or restaurant meal.

Managers oversee the work of these people, coordinating a variety of services including housekeeping, kitchen staff, marketing, inventory control, bookkeeping, and human resources. But they're not just behind-the-scenes people. Hotel and restaurant managers are generally "people people." They love contact with their guests, and enjoy providing the kind of customer service that brings people back to their establishments over and over again. This book introduces you to these exciting careers, in which you might find yourself working for a huge city hotel, an ocean-side resort, a contract food service company, an ethnic restaurant, or one of hundreds of other employers.

Chapter 1 serves as a general exploration of the field. In it, you will learn what hotel and restaurant managers do, where they work, and what makes them successful. Also included are hiring trends and current salary information, sample job descriptions, and advice from current hotel and restaurant managers.

Chapter 2 explains the importance of training, and how to decide what kind of post-secondary education is right for you. It explains the different types of programs and how to succeed once you have entered one. Sample courses and tuition costs from schools across the country are also in this chapter.

In Chapter 3, you will learn the possibilities for financing your education, including loans, scholarships, and grants. The differences between each option are explored, explaining eligibility, the application process, and how awards are given. You will also find out about the forms you need, where to get them, how to fill them out, and where to send them, and get some tips for simplifying and surviving the process.

Chapter 4 covers the job search process, beginning with a discussion about determining the type of job you really want. There is plenty of information on where the best jobs are, and the best ways to find them, from classified ads to networking and Internet resources.

Then, in Chapter 5, you will learn how to hone your job search skills. The crafting of winning resumes and cover letters that really get noticed is explained, along with advice on how to handle interviews with more polish and less anxiety. Finally, you will learn how to evaluate the job offers you are sure to receive.

Chapter 6 takes you out of the job search and into the job market, showing proven ways to succeed in your new position. You will learn how to manage relationships with your superiors and your employees, as well as how to handle the stress that often accompanies work as a hotel or restaurant manager. Other topics covered include fitting into the particular culture of your new workplace, how to find a mentor, and how to promote yourself to get ahead.

In addition, throughout the book, you will find insight and advice from current hotel and restaurant managers. The appendices at the end of the book offer helpful resources too: A list of professional associations, accrediting agencies, and state financial aid offices, as well as a directory of training programs. Also included are books and periodicals you can refer to for additional information.

So, turn the page and begin. This book will give you a great start toward a rewarding and challenging career as a hotel or restaurant manager.

HOTEL/RESTAURANT MANAGEMENT
CAREER STARTER

CHAPTER one

CHOOSING A CAREER AS A HOTEL OR RESTAURANT MANAGER

IN THIS CHAPTER, you will learn about hotel and restaurant managers, including what they do, where they work, and what makes them successful. Jobs with large hotels and restaurants, resorts, healthcare facilities, and contract food service companies are examined, along with sample job advertisements from many of these employers. You will also hear advice from a number of those already working in the field. Finally, the specific strengths and skills necessary to succeed as a hotel or restaurant manager will be explored in an interactive format.

THE CAREERS of both hotel and restaurant managers are part of the hospitality industry. This means that they revolve around making people feel comfortable and welcome, and meeting their needs—whether for a great meal at a reasonable price, or for a clean, comfortable room for the night. Hotel and restaurant managers, and indeed all who work in the hospitality industry, thrive on making their guests happy and enjoy contact with many different people. They also juggle a variety of responsibilities. While they have staffs that work for them, ultimately it is the manager who takes the praise or blame for the way a hotel or restaurant is run.

WHAT IS A HOTEL OR RESTAURANT MANAGER?

Hotel managers are executives who work at various types of lodging establishments, such as large chain hotels, smaller independent hotels, inns, resorts, and even on cruise ships. Most have received training in the form of an undergraduate degree in hospitality management, and have then worked their way up through the ranks to the position of manager. They run their establishments by coordinating a number of different services, including the front desk, reservations, housekeeping, maintenance, and marketing. Depending on the employer, a hotel manager may have assistant managers to help with these services, or may be solely responsible for them. Since a hotel is typically open every day of the year, and services are provided 24 hours a day, a manager rarely works a 40-hour week. Alternative titles for hotel managers include:

- ▶ General Manager
- ▶ Hotelier
- ▶ Convention Facility Manager
- ▶ Tourist Hotel Manager
- ▶ Manager (Hotel)
- ▶ Operations Manager (Hotel)

Restaurant or food service managers also work at various types of establishments, from large chain restaurants, to healthcare facilities and contract food service companies. While many restaurant managers hold undergraduate degrees in hospitality management, it is possible to advance to this position through a combination of job experience and employer training programs. The manager is in charge of the smooth operation of the dining establishment—coordinating all of the services involved in the business, including bookkeeping, human resources, marketing, menu choices and pricing, maintenance, ordering of supplies, and kitchen management. In large restaurants, the manager may oversee the work of a number of assistant managers, who deal with much of the hands-on operation; however, in smaller restaurants, the manager may be personally involved in every aspect of the enterprise. In addition, most dining facilities are open seven days a week, meaning that a manager can expect to work long hours and on weekends.

WHAT DO HOTEL AND RESTAURANT MANAGERS DO?

Hotel managers plan, organize, and control the operation of a hotel or other lodging facility. The size and type of the hotel at which the manager is employed helps determine the scope of the manager's duties. Large hotels are headed by general managers, whose jobs are primarily administrative. If the hotel is part of a chain, the general manager works for the corporate officers, and may have many activities, such as purchasing or marketing, performed by the corporation.

General managers typically delegate many responsibilities to their managers, and coordinate the various departments within the hotel. For instance, the convention department, headed by the convention manager, organizes and coordinates services for meetings to be held in the hotel; the marketing and sales department, staffed with salespeople, promotes the hotel and its services to achieve a high rate of use; the food service department coordinates menu planning, purchasing and the preparation of food; the human resources department makes hiring and firing decisions; the front office handles room reservations and greets guests; and the housekeeping department is comprised of a cleaning staff and is in charge of the maintenance of the rooms and lobby areas. Many large hotels also have recreational managers who provide, or otherwise make available to, guests a variety of activities.

Managers who work in small or medium-sized hotels have a more hands-on, rather than administrative, position. Instead of heading up a number of departments which are led by employees who report to them, these managers take a direct role in activities such as hiring and firing, menu planning and food preparation, and marketing of the hotel. Managers of smaller lodging facilities may also fill in when there are gaps in the staff or services; they might greet guests at the front desk, inspect rooms, or set up function rooms for meetings. Many of them are also owners or part-owners of the establishments in which they work.

In general, however, there are many tasks and duties shared by hotel managers whether they work on a cruise ship or a mountain lodge, a 1,000-room city hotel, or a bed and breakfast in a college town. They include:

▶ managing the hotel's business plan or direction
▶ hiring and training new staff
▶ handling requests and complaints from guests
▶ keeping records, planning budgets, and dealing with accounts
▶ advertising the hotel and dealing with tour operators
▶ supervising the day-to-day running of the hotel
▶ taking bookings, greeting guests, and allocating rooms
▶ devising the annual business plan for the hotel
▶ having final say in quality and cost control

Restaurant managers are in charge of the food and service at a variety of settings, including restaurants, hotel dining rooms, catering facilities, healthcare sites, schools and other institutions. Depending on the employer, a restaurant manager oversees all aspects of the operation, from choosing the items that appear on the menu, to hiring and managing staff, to dealing with record-keeping and payroll. As with hotel managers, the duties of the restaurant manager rely somewhat on the type of establishment where he or she is employed.

At large chain restaurants, the corporate owners make many of the decisions regarding the operation of their facilities. They may plan the menus, coordinate the suppliers of food, beverages, and other items, design the décor, implement a marketing plan, and even determine the size and scheduling of the staff. The manager of such a restaurant is thoroughly trained by the corporation and is expected to run the facility within strict corporate guidelines.

Smaller restaurants give more responsibility to their managers. Instead of having decisions made by corporate officers, most, if not all, of the decisions are made in-house specifically for that restaurant. The manager of a smaller restaurant must take a hands-on approach to the job, working with the kitchen staff, the host or hostess, and the wait staff closely. When something goes wrong, such as equipment failure, short staffing, or food spoilage, the manager must step in and solve the problem.

No matter what the size of the restaurant, however, a food service manager's duties typically include:

- ▶ overseeing food preparation and cooking
- ▶ checking food quality and portion size to ensure that dishes are prepared and garnished correctly and in a timely manner
- ▶ investigating and resolving customer complaints about food and service
- ▶ continually monitoring workers and observing patrons
- ▶ ordering supplies, such as food, beverages, linens, tableware, and fixtures
- ▶ interviewing, hiring, and firing employees
- ▶ daily tallying cash and charge receipts received and comparing them with records of sales or budgeted figures
- ▶ assuring compliance with health and safety regulations
- ▶ scheduling the work shifts of employees

WHAT MAKES A GREAT HOTEL OR RESTAURANT MANAGER?

Those who hire hotel and restaurant managers, while always looking for employees with the proper educational background, emphasize the individual skills necessary for success in these careers. Hotel managers need to have strong initiative, good leadership and decision-making abilities, and planning and organizational skills. They must show proficiency in administrative, financial, marketing, and business management duties. They also need to be self-disciplined and have excellent communication and people skills as well as some knowledge of computers. Managers of small hotels may also need to be familiar with basic electrical, mechanical, and plumbing services.

The people skills an employer looks for in hotel managers include maturity and responsibility, friendliness, patience, and helpfulness. Good judgment and clear thinking are crucial considering the often stressful nature of the job. Emergencies, as well as the occasional irate guest, must be dealt with calmly and efficiently.

Hotel managers should know about health and safety regulations, tourist attractions in the area, and liquor licensing regulations. They need to be able to coordinate a number of different functions and work well under pressure. They should have some knowledge of other cultures and be sensitive to the diverse needs of their guests. In order to remain successful, hotel managers must be willing to keep up-to-date with new developments in the industry and their local market.

The qualities most sought after in restaurant managers are very similar to those for hotel managers. For example, self-discipline, initiative, and leadership ability are essential. Food service managers must be detail-oriented and able to solve problems. They need good communication and interpersonal skills to deal with customers, suppliers, and their staff. Food safety and sanitation regulations must be learned and strictly adhered to. Maximizing profit while minimizing all types of waste is essential in a business where the profit margin is quite small to begin with. Restaurant managers must be on top of every aspect of the operation of their facility to keep it financially viable.

The stress level for restaurant managers can be high, and therefore they need to be able to think clearly and deal with problems quickly and successfully. Long hours—many of them spent on their feet—means that good general health is also necessary for restaurant managers.

HIRING TRENDS AND SALARIES

The hospitality industry is a major employer in the United States labor market, and is projected to grow as such through 2010. Currently, the restaurant industry employs more than 11.3 million people; food service managers accounted for over 465,000 of those jobs in 2000. The lodging industry employs 7.8 million; in 2000, it experienced the best year in its history, bringing in double the profits seen in 1996.

There are a number of factors affecting projections of future employment of hotel and restaurant managers. In the lodging industry, the trend toward industry consolidation, with large corporations buying independently owned establishments, decreases the number of managers needed overall. However, the increasing amount of business travel creates the need for more full-service hotels, which provide the greatest number of management positions. A high turnover rate in the industry also accounts for many opportunities for those entering the job market. Employers continue to primarily seek out those with two- or four-year degrees in hospitality management.

Restaurant management positions across the country are expected to increase by 10% to 20% through 2010. However, this percentage will be much higher in large cities and tourist destinations. For example, the California Labor Market Information Division projects that, in its state alone, there will be a 45% increase in the number of restaurant managers through 2005. This growth rate is almost twice the average for all occupations in the state. Most new restaurant management jobs will come from the increasing number of dining establishments which cater to an ever-expanding population. More and more schools, hospitals, company dining rooms, and airports are contracting out food services, creating a large number of new positions for restaurant and food service managers.

Another trend affecting the employment of restaurant managers is the dominance of national chain restaurants over independent ones. More new restaurants are corporately owned, which means that the owner can't be the manager, as was frequently the case in independently owned restaurants. Corporations such as Darden Restaurants (which owns Red Lobster and Olive Garden) and Brinker International (Chili's Grill and Bar, Romano's Macaroni Grill) employ thousands of managers to run their operations across the country.

According to the Bureau of Labor Statistics, the median annual income of hotel managers and assistants was $26,700 in 2000. The wide range of salaries varies based on the job responsibilities of the manager and the area of the hospitality industry in which he or she works. Many large, full-service hotels routinely pay managers bonuses of up to 25 percent of their salaries. Benefits may include such services as lodging, meals, parking, and laundry, which can add up to substantial financial rewards. In addition, profit-sharing, retirement plans, stock purchasing options, and tuition reimbursement are also part of the compensation packages of many employers.

The American Hotel and Lodging Association's Education Institute reports current average salaries as follows:

Reservations Manager $31,100
Executive Housekeeper $31,550
Front Office Manager $33,900

Catering Sales Manager $35,600
Sales Manager $37,000
Chief Engineer $49,000
Human Resources Director $49,000
Senior Sales Manager $51,100
Controller $57,100
Food and Beverage Director $62,400
Director of Sales and Marketing $70,100
General Manager (non live-in) $97,300
General Manager $108,487

The Bureau of Labor Statistics reports that food service managers earned an average of $31,720 in 2000, with the middle 50% earning between $24,500 and $41,000. Their *Occupational Outlook Handbook* also breaks down earnings by industry, as follows:

Miscellaneous amusement and recreation services $37,000
Hotels and motels $36,460
Nursing and personal care facilities $31,400
Eating and drinking places $31,380
Elementary and secondary schools $28,310

Benefits for restaurant managers vary with employers. The best packages are usually offered by large employers such as corporations, which reward their employees with profit-sharing plans, retirement savings plans, tuition reimbursement, and comprehensive insurance coverage. In addition to such typical benefits, many restaurant and food service managers are given free meals and the opportunity for additional training.

According to a recent National Restaurant Association compensation survey, median annual salaries and bonuses (in parentheses) for food service managers are as follows:

Banquet Manager $32,000 ($3,000)
Catering Manager $35,000 ($4,000)
Unit Manager $35,132 ($4,615)
Assistant Unit Manager $28,000 ($2,460)

Night Manager $26,000 ($1,500)
Manager Trainee $25,080 ($2,000)
Dining Room Manager $30,000 ($2,000)
Kitchen Manager $29,000 ($2,000)
Regional Manager $62,500 ($15,000)
District Manager $53,262 ($10,000)
Regional Training Manager   50,914 ($4,318)

THE IMPORTANCE OF TRAINING

As with many other professions, the current hiring trend in hotels and restaurants is to seek candidates with postsecondary training. Previously, many managers worked their way up through the ranks, learning everything they needed to know on the job before landing a position as manager. Now, however, many hotels and restaurants are owned by large corporations. These corporate employers want to make certain every establishment they hold is a financial success, and they begin by selectively hiring managers and management trainees who have studied the business of hospitality in college. In fact, most food service management companies and national or regional restaurant and hotel chains recruit management trainees directly from two- and four-year college hospitality management programs.

A large number of colleges and universities offer four-year programs in restaurant and hotel management or institutional food service management. If a four-year program won't work for you for some reason, community and junior colleges, technical institutes, and other institutions offer similar courses of study. These alternatives may lead to an associate degree or other formal certification. Chapter 2 explains the differences between these different programs, and advice on how to choose one. In addition, you will find a listing of schools around the country that offer hospitality management training in Appendix C.

One of the reasons hospitality employers prefer job candidates with college degrees is that these candidates not only have knowledge and skills learned in the classroom, but often graduate with a variety of work experiences as well. Most hotel and restaurant management programs require students to complete internships working in actual hotels or restaurants for college credit. Many also run their own hotel or restaurant right on or near by the campus, affording even greater hands-on, work-study learning opportunities.

Todd Warren, who holds a degree in hospitality management, explains the benefits of a work-study program:

> To the degree you can juggle your schedule, get as much work experience as you can while in school. I worked every year in college, and graduated with a four-year head start over my classmates. Some of them had never held a position in a hotel or restaurant, and entered the job market looking for a management opening.

There are a number of other advantages to be gained by the job candidate with post-secondary training in hospitality management. Many schools hire those working in the industry to teach their classes, putting their students in contact with potential employers right away. Colleges and universities are frequently the sites of job fairs, where employers gather to interview and hire graduating seniors. They also maintain relationships with area businesses that hire their graduates, and thus become an invaluable resource for job hunters.

All of this doesn't mean you won't be able to find a job if you haven't or can't go to college, but that you may have a more difficult time than someone with a degree in hand. Because formal training is so important, we have devoted two entire chapters of this book to the subject of your education and how to pay for it. As you read through Chapter 2, remain flexible regarding your ideas about education. You may think now that you would like to jump into the job market right out of high school (and that may still be your course of action after reading this book), but be willing to consider other options. There are programs that take just a year to complete, and they offer some of the same benefits as longer programs.

If you haven't considered education beyond high school because you have always felt you couldn't afford it, Chapter 3 will take you through the financial aid "marketplace," explaining the types of aid available, where they can be found, and how and when to apply. However, if you didn't graduate from high school, your first step is to get a General Educational Development

Certificate, or GED. In most states, you must complete a battery of tests in math, reading, grammar (including writing skills), social studies, and science. In addition to knowledge in these subject areas, you may be asked to document instruction in health, civic literacy, and career education.

To prepare for the GED tests, you can sign up for classes or individualized study offered in many communities through adult schools and non-profit agencies. Public television series often offer study materials, and you can receive educational support through phone contact and occasional teacher/student face-to-face meetings on campus. Technical colleges also offer these services and are often official GED test sites. Some states recognize the "life experience" of adults who did not graduate from high school, but who have learned skills equivalent to those expected of high school graduates. They evaluate and give credit for skills learned on the job, through raising a family, or from one's own self-directed learning. Check with your state's higher education department, listed in Appendix C, for more information about obtaining a GED in your area.

WHERE DO HOTEL AND RESTAURANT MANAGERS WORK?

Once you enter the workforce, your overall job satisfaction will depend largely on how well you like the environment provided by your employer. Therefore, it is critical that you give consideration not only to the type of job you would like to have, but where and for whom you would like to work. There are big differences between contract food service companies and small, family-owned restaurants, between large, thousand-room hotels and quaint country inns.

Employment opportunities for hotel and restaurant managers may be found throughout the country, with a higher concentration in large cities and tourist destinations. While it is impossible to summarize all of the various work environments of hotel and restaurant managers, a description of some of the largest employers follows, including some advantages and disadvantages of each. You will also find recent job advertisements for positions with these types of employers. While reading the following descriptions, keep in mind your reactions to each; you may already believe you know the type of employer you prefer, but may not be aware of the scope of opportunities available. For more information about these and other workplaces, see Chapter 6.

Corporations and Large Businesses

Corporations are, because of their size, hierarchical. You will find in these organizations that there are often senior-level managers, who supervise junior-level managers, who supervise a staff of other employees. There are advantages and disadvantages to working in such a setting. To begin with, you will be presented with a clear path for your career, including possibilities for raises and promotions.

The Top Five Brands in the Hotel Industry:

Cendant Corporation

6,105 properties in the United States, including Ramada, Days Inn, Howard Johnson's, and Fairfield Inn

Choice Hotels International

3,915 properties in the United States, including Comfort Inn, Quality Inn, Econo Lodge, and Clarion Hotel

Bass Hotels and Resorts

2,202 properties in the United States, including Holiday Inn, Crowne Plaza, and Inter-Continental

Best Western

2,116 properties in the United States

Hilton Hotel Corporation

1,864 properties in the United States, including Hampton Inn, Hilton Hotel, and Embassy Suites

Corporations have many resources that smaller companies don't, so they can offer more to their employees. If you are interested in continuing your education, you may find that your employer will pay some or all of the cost associated with attending seminars, preparing for certification exams (see the section on certification), or obtaining a college degree. You may also find that working for a corporation will provide:

▶ a higher salary
▶ better benefits—more days of sick leave and vacation, superior insurance, and retirement programs
▶ greater opportunity for advancement if the hierarchy is not too rigid—at any rate, greater opportunity within your category
▶ more departments to transfer into if the one you are in doesn't suit you
▶ better equipment, so your job will be easier and you can be more creative

On the downside, some people feel suffocated by the hierarchy of corporations. Your job description will be very clear and there will most likely be little opportunity to stray from it. Free-spirited types may find it difficult to fit into the corporate culture, which is typically conservative and somewhat formal. Other drawbacks can include:

▶ a more conservative set of rules
▶ less variety in the work because of the large, usually specialized work force
▶ sometimes less chance for advancement, if the hierarchy is extremely rigid
▶ a more impersonal atmosphere
▶ the need to spend more money on clothing

Largest Brands in the Restaurant Industry by Revenue in the Year 2000 in Millions

McDonald's: $14,243

Tricon Global (Kentucky Fried Chicken, Pizza Hut, Taco Bell): $7,093

Darden Restaurants, Inc. (Red Lobster, Olive Garden): $3,701

Wendy's International: $2,234

Brinker International (Chili's Grill and Bar, Romano's Macaroni Grill, On the Border
    Mexican Cantina): $2,160

Outback Steakhouse, Inc.: $1,906

Sample Job Advertisement

Star Corporation is seeking Restaurant Managers for our operations in and around the St. Louis area. We offer excellent salaries, wonderful benefits, and the opportunity to advance in a supportive, performance-based environment. As a manager, you will:

- provide leadership by example, working alongside your team to reach company objectives
- operate in accordance with established performance, profit and operating standards, as set out in the company manual
- assume responsibility for all facets of operations for one of our restaurants, working a minimum of 45 hours per week
- maintain and meet our high standards of cleanliness and customer service
- purchase food, beverages, and supplies as needed, and oversee their preparation to ensure that our standards of product quality are met
- hire and train employees, assign and schedule duties, and assist in employee development
- review individual performance of employees and assistant managers; recommend salary/wage adjustments as appropriate

Our benefit package includes a competitive starting salary with periodic review; 401(k) retirement savings plan; comprehensive health insurance; group dental insurance; short-term disability; life and long-term disability insurance; tuition reimbursement; stock purchase plan; paid vacations; software training; employee discounts; and meal reimbursement.

Independent Hotels and Restaurants

There are thousands of hotels and restaurants that are not owned by large corporations. They exist in every major city, and most towns as well. They may be found in resort areas, near colleges and universities, and in out-of-the way villages. This category includes both large restaurants bringing in millions of dollars a year and pizzerias; there are also thousand-room hotels in big cities and bed-and-breakfasts in the mountains. But, all of these facilities have something in common—they are not owned or run by huge corporations.

Working for a smaller organization can offer a number of advantages over working for a larger one. They may include a more relaxed work atmosphere, and the chance to perform duties not necessarily in your job description. Whereas in a corporately owned facility every phase of operation is dictated by upper management, there is more room for flexibility and creativity for managers in independently owned hotels and restaurants. In addition, you may find a personal, less formal setting, in which individuals are respected for their unique qualities. Independently owned hotels and restaurants tend toward a teamlike atmosphere. If one person is successful everyone shares the success. You will find, in such a setting, a pleasant working environment that promotes growth and cooperation.

However, you may also find lower pay, fewer benefits, and less than state-of-the-art technology. In some smaller hotels and restaurants, there is little chance for advancement simply because there aren't enough job openings to move up into. In addition, there could be less job stability as smaller operations fight to stay afloat in economic downturns that might be weathered more easily by large companies. Many are willing to put up with the disadvantages, though, as a trade-off for the many rewards to be had from this type of employer.

Sample Job Advertisements

RESTAURANT MANAGER. Pomegranate, a 40-seat restaurant located in DC, Washingtonian top 100 and 3-star chef, is searching for a manager. Applicant should have fine dining experience—any wine knowledge is a plus. Candidate should also possess good organizational skills and be detail oriented, personable, and comfortable supervising servers and support staff. Other job responsibilities include scheduling, hiring, training, inventory control, reservations, implementing new systems, and maintaining an efficient dining room. Salary is negotiable plus benefits.

Do you have a flair for living and a taste for fun? The Silver Kettle Restaurant is looking for a Manager. A unique restaurant open for dinner only, the Silver Kettle is an upscale, but casually elegant, dining destination.

As Manager you will be responsible for the daily operations of the restaurant: training of staff and overseeing the kitchen, serving, hosting, and bartending stations. You will be responsible for cost of sales, labor cost, and proper ordering. You will also need to retain guest counts, ensure guest satisfaction, and motivate employees. The Silver Kettle offers a fixed, five-day work week, free meals, medical benefits, paid vacations, holidays, and other added incentives. Salary from $29,000, commensurate with experience.

Resort and Clubs

Most of these facilities are owned and operated by large companies, making them similar in many ways to corporately owned hotels and restaurants. However, they differ in a few important aspects. First, they cater exclusively to guests who are enjoying leisure time, either for an evening or a week-long vacation. That doesn't mean you won't run into an irate guest or two, but, for the most part, the atmosphere is heightened by the guests' eagerness to enjoy themselves. Second, being employed by a resort can result in a great lifestyle. For instance, if you love to ski, you may find work at a mountain lodge, where you can enjoy your sport for free during off hours. If you prefer warm climates, employment at a beach resort means you can live year round in the sun.

Darby Crum, a restaurant manager in Vermont, says:

> I wanted to become a resort restaurant manager because I love the vacation atmosphere. I've always gotten along well with people, and wanted to be around a lot of them in an exciting setting. I also love to ski, so working at a ski resort seemed like a natural fit for me.

Check out the section in Chapter 4 on the Resort Industry if this type of position appeals to you. There you will find valuable information on employers such as casinos and cruise lines, and great Internet sites on which to conduct further research.

Sample Job Advertisement

A successful, rapidly expanding casino and entertainment company seeks an experienced Beverage Manager. This position is responsible for the planning, development, and implementation of procedures to improve the efficiency of the Food and Beverage areas. Must prepare annual budget, variance reports, weekly management reports, comp reports, and linen/glass/silver/menu inventory. This position involves work in pricing, quality, marketing, customer satisfaction, and employee training and development. Qualified candidate will have a demonstrated track record of successfully increasing revenue after the introduction and management of numerous innovative ideas/processes, while maintaining employee morale. The qualified candidate will possess a College degree in Business, or related Food and Beverage field. A thorough knowledge of all aspects of food and beverage operations pertaining to a hotel/casino or property of this size is preferred. Salary from $34,000.

Contract Food Service Companies

These employers supply entire food service packages, including chefs, vending machines, servers, management, and the food itself, to a variety of facilities, including government agencies and offices, corporate dining rooms, airports, schools, and hospitals. Since they are all fairly large corporations, working for one of them will be similar in terms of advantages and disadvantages to working for a corporately-owned restaurant.

Contract food service management companies hire employees to fill many of the same types of positions that restaurants do. They need servers, kitchen staff, bookkeepers, and managers to run their various operations. Because of the corporate hierarchy, restaurant managers and assistant managers report in to a general manager who is usually assigned a district, or group of locations, to run; they then report to higher level management, which reports to the corporate officers. The largest employers in this group include Sodexho Alliance, Aramark, and Compass Group. Find out more about them, and the contract food service business, by checking out their websites: www.sodexhousa.com, www.aramark.com, and www.compassgroup.com. You can also search the Internet with the term "contract food service" for more information.

Healthcare Facilities

This is one of the fastest growing employers for the hospitality industry, due in part to the aging population and its increasing need for healthcare. As medical science improves our quality and length of life, and as treatments are found for previously untreatable ailments, more and more people are finding themselves in short- or long-term care facilities, hospitals, and nursing homes.

While some healthcare facilities use contract food service operators (see the previous section), many do not, preferring to handle their food service in-house. They hire food service managers to oversee the implementation of this service from purchasing and staffing, to menu planning and distribution of meals that take into account the various needs of their populations. In addition, many of these facilities also employ the equivalent of hotel managers to direct their housekeeping, "reservations," maintenance, and other departments.

Sample Job Advertisements

Major contract food service corporation seeks Food Service Director for a large university cafeteria. Major responsibilities include client, student and employee relations, financial management, and menu planning and execution. The ideal candidate will be an innovative, involved, goal-oriented leader with strong organizational, communication and people skills. Excellent benefits package and opportunity for advancement within the company.

Assistant Manager, college food service. Reports to general manager. Responsibilities include customer and client relations, management of a busy dining room, unit sanitation, assisting the catering area, purchasing cleaning supplies, assisting with ongoing inventories, supervising employees, and other special projects. This position requires a minimum of two years supervisory experience in the Healthcare or College Food Service Industry.

OPPORTUNITIES FOR ADVANCEMENT

There are two basic avenues to career advancement for hotel and restaurant managers. The first is to find employment with a large organization that is known for promoting from within, and has a sizeable chain of command through which you can rise. The other is to move from employer to employer as you either rise laterally through management ranks or seek different positions that utilize your skills and offer better pay, better hours, or some other advantage.

Those who get promoted have a few basic characteristics in common. They know their employer's business, and constantly seek out new information about how it is run and its current state of operation. These managers understand the company philosophy and follow dictated procedures closely. They not only play by the rules, they know the rules inside out.

Getting a promotion depends heavily on attitude. You need to stress customer service—showing genuine care for guests and fellow employees—consistently. A positive attitude toward the constant changes that are inherent in the hospitality industry is also essential. An employer doesn't respond well to an employee who gripes about his or her job; you will need to embrace the changes that upper management mandates, and show that you are a team player. Employees who rise up through the ranks of management also take the time, even when they begin their careers as management trainees, to get to know their superiors in their companies. Make an effort early on to make contact with upper management, and make a positive impression.

Generally speaking, large hotel and restaurant chains offer better opportunities for advancement than small, independently owned establishments, but may require periodic relocation in order to keep moving ahead. These companies have large ranks, and can offer a manager the chance to move to a larger facility in the chain, or even to the corporate offices.

If your first position is with a smaller organization that has no room for you to advance, and you have outgrown that position, you will need to seek your next job with another employer who has a suitable opening. This means, for example, that a dining room manager at a small hotel might apply for a position as a general manager, catering manager, or district manager of a large chain operation. The manager of a 200-room hotel might move to a similar position at a 1,000-room hotel. Or, you might look to another type of business, such as hospitality consulting, which can benefit from your experience and provide you with growth opportunities.

When you feel you are ready to advance, don't wait for a superior to suggest a promotion. Be proactive about your career by applying for a job with more responsibility and a higher salary, a job working for a higher-level supervisor within your organization, or a more challenging job with another firm or organization. In Chapter 6, there is more information about the process of promoting yourself and changing jobs.

CERTIFICATION

There are a number of professional certifications available to hotel or restaurant managers. Most require job experience before taking the qualifying exam, but some will substitute a college degree for experience. The possible advantages of obtaining certification include:

▶ distinguishing yourself from the crowd when applying for a job or seeking a promotion

▶ gaining further education through preparation for the exam(s)

▶ receiving a higher salary than those professionals without certification

▶ demonstrating to your employer that you are a professional and committed to advancing your career

▶ receiving college credit (many colleges and universities offer course credit for passing certification exams)

Sample Job Advertisement

Food Service Supervisor, State University Health System. Responsible for the supervision, training, and evaluation of employees in the area and shift assigned to. Accountable for maintaining operation in accordance with hospital and department policies. Ensures regulatory compliance at all times; directs, evaluates, and schedules employees in areas as required. The food service supervisor also maintains schedules for employees; assigns employees to perform tasks; and checks all food items for appearance, flavor, texture, portion size and temperature to ensure compliance with patient diet and menu orders, catering, and cafeteria menu offerings.

Education and experience should include completion of high school with either the 90-hour certificate in food service management or equivalent experience as a food service supervisor. Two-year Associate degree or B.S. in food service management or related field preferred.

The American Hotel and Lodging Association (AH&LA) currently offers 20 different certifications for employees ranging from corporate executives to housekeeping staff. The most popular is the Certified Lodging Manager designation. It may be achieved through one of three plans, each of which requires successful completion of an exam. Plan A is for those applicants who have more education than experience. It requires just two years of experience, current employment as a manager of a lodging establishment, and at least a two-year hospitality degree from an accredited institution (successful completion of the Educational Institute's Hospitality Management Diploma may be substituted).

Plan B emphasizes experience over education. To be eligible, you must have at least three years of management experience, and be currently employed as a lodging manager. Plan C is for those applicants with little experience, either with or without a hospitality degree. It allows the applicant to take the exam after accruing a specified number of "professional development points." For those without a degree, the number of points needed is determined by first subtracting the number of months employed in a qualifying position from 36; for those with a degree, subtract the number of months employed from 24. Then, the number of months is divided by two. Points are earned through activities such as taking (and passing) undergraduate hospitality courses, completing a professional development seminar, and passing an Educational Institute distance learning course.

There are also a large number of professional certifications available to those working as restaurant and food service managers. They range from specialized designations geared toward compliance with state and local food safety laws such as sanitation, to more general certifications. Many are offered through the Educational Foundation of the National Restaurant Association (NRA), including the certified Foodservice Management Professional (FMP) designation. While signifying a level of professional achievement, this certification has no advanced degree requirement, making those who were educated primarily on the job eligible. It is awarded after the applicant passes a written exam, completes a series of courses, and meets work experience requirements.

Professional certifications for hotel and restaurant managers are typically valid for five years. After this period, those holding designations must provide proof of continuing education in order to keep the certification current. The same associations that award professional designations also provide many opportunities for continuing education, including online courses, seminars, and publications.

SKILLS INVENTORY

You have read about what a hotel or restaurant manager is, and what he or she does. You have learned where they work and how they can get ahead in their careers. Now, you can determine whether you are ready to seek a position as a hotel or restaurant manager. This questionnaire was designed to get you thinking about the skills necessary to succeed on the job, including those you already possess, and those you may want to work on developing. It is a good idea to understand your strengths and weaknesses before you enter the job market, when there is plenty of time to turn your weaknesses around.

Read the following statements, determine your honest answer, and then circle true or false for each.

1. I enjoy fast-paced environments and work best under pressure.   T   F

2. I like doing one thing at a time, completing each task before moving on to the next.   T   F

3. When faced with criticism, I usually get defensive.   T   F

4. In an emergency or crisis situation, I keep a level head and take charge.   T   F

5. I love the town I live in and would not like to relocate for my job.   T   F

6. I am good at managing people and bringing out the best in them.   T   F

7. I am interested in food trends and love to experiment with new recipes.   T   F

8. Making people feel welcome and at home is important to me.   T   F

9. I like working for someone who gives plenty of direction.   T   F

10. Computers and other technology don't interest me.   T   F

11. My family is very understanding about the demands of my job.   T   F

12. I am very patient.   T   F

13. Details bore me; I'd rather work on the big picture.   T   F

14. I don't want to make mistakes, so I prefer to wait until I understand exactly what is expected of me before proceeding with any task.   T   F

15. I like a clean house, and don't mind spending extra time to keep mine that way.   T   F

16. I get bored when I have to do the same thing every   T   F
    day; change keeps me energized.

Take note of your answers. The questionnaire is not an absolute measure of your suitability, but if you answered "true" to statements 1, 4, 6, 7, 8, 11, 12, 15, and 16, you already possess many of the skills necessary for success as a hotel or restaurant manager. If you answered "false" to any of these statements, begin thinking about ways to improve your skills. Education in hospitality management will help with some of them, as will an affiliation with one or more of the various industry associations. Remember, you will want to become the best possible job candidate you can be before making contact with potential employers.

Read on to discover how to prepare for your career as a hotel or restaurant manager. In the next chapters, you will learn how to get the education you need, how to pay for it, and how to get the most out of it. Then, discover where the hotel and restaurant management jobs are, and how to find and succeed in one.

THE INSIDE TRACK

Who:	Dina Guzman
What:	Hotel Manager
Where:	La Tierra Lodge
	Santa Fe, New Mexico

INSIDER'S STORY

I started my career in hospitality during high school. I grew up in a resort town in southern California, and my first jobs were all in restaurants and hotels. I was really young, so I started out cleaning hotel rooms and busing tables. The work itself wasn't always fun, but I did like the atmosphere. I was especially attracted to hotel work—the guests were always so excited to be there.

When I went away to college, I initially planned to study biology, but I found myself losing interest in it. A friend of mine was in the hospitality program and the more she talked about the things she was learning, the more it sounded like something I'd like to be involved with. I switched my major to hospitality when I was a junior. During my senior year, I did a professional internship with a hotel manager at a huge chain hotel. That was a big eye-opener for me. I'd learned in my courses about how much work a management job was, but it was very different to spend whole days with the manager, seeing how much paper and how many people went in and out of her office in a day.

I graduated from the University of California at San Diego with a Bachelor of Science in Hospitality, specializing in hotel management. After graduation, I went to work for the same hotel chain I had interned for. I started as a front desk supervisor and was promoted to Night Manager after six months. I really enjoyed that position; I had a lot of opportunities to interact with the guests, and I actually liked working at night, since the pace of the hotel calmed down slightly.

After two years, I was promoted to Assistant General Manager, and then three years later, to General Manager of another hotel owned by the same company. A general manager in a hotel this size is really more of a coordinating person; all of the different departments reported to me, and I in turn reported to a regional manager. I made all of the decisions about day-to-day operations, but after a while, I started to feel like I was missing out on the best part of the business by being in a position that was so overwhelmingly made up of administrative work. I have always thought of myself as a "people person," and I missed having direct contact with the hotel's guests.

Choosing a Career as a Hotel or Restaurant Manager

I had worked in that position for nearly ten years when my husband and I decided to open our own boutique hotel. Leaving a company I'd grown so used to working for was a big change, and it's not easy to get a small business off the ground. But it's been five years now and I'm so glad to be doing this. We run a small hotel (10 rooms) and employ just a few people as night clerks and cleaners. My husband was an accountant in his previous job, so he deals with most of the finances. It works out nicely for me, because I get a chance to really take care of our guests. I oversee everything from reservations, to recommending restaurants and places to go, to occasionally changing light bulbs or vacuuming.

I wish I had had a sense earlier in my career of what a broad variety of positions were available in this field. It's easy to get comfortable in one place and stay there, but if I hadn't been willing to leave a safe job and take a risk, I wouldn't feel nearly as rewarded by my work as I do today. My advice is to keep up with industry trends and explore other properties whenever the chance presents itself. Knowing what your options are is important to a satisfying career.

CHAPTER two

GETTING THE EDUCATION YOU NEED

IN THIS CHAPTER, you will learn why formal training is important. You will explore the types of educational opportunities available, including sample courses and tuition costs from schools around the country. You will discover how to choose a training program by evaluating not only the program, but your needs as well. Finally, you can review some tips on succeeding once you're enrolled and learn how to land an internship and how to prepare for exams.

THE United States Department of Labor reports that jobs in the hotel industry will grow more slowly than average through 2008, while those in restaurant management will grow at an average rate. However, for those with formal training (the Department of Labor stresses a two- or four-year degree), employment prospects are great. Surveys of employers agree with these findings—most employees on the management staff in large hotel and restaurant chains hold associate or bachelor's degrees.

The lesson here is that while some do indeed rise up through the ranks with just a high school diploma, the possibility of doing so will diminish in the coming years. As the industry becomes more competitive and diverse, the need for highly qualified, educated employees increases. A degree or certificate in hotel or restaurant management will get you hired more quickly when entering the job market and increase your chances for promotion throughout your career.

You won't have to look far for your education. In 1998, nearly 200 community and junior colleges and some universities offered associate, bachelor's, and graduate degree programs in hotel or restaurant management. When combined with technical institutes, vocational and trade schools, and other academic institutions, over 800 educational facilities have programs leading to formal recognition in hotel or restaurant management.

WHY YOU NEED TRAINING

We have stressed the importance of entering the job market with a degree, or at least a certificate, in hand. But it is not just the piece of paper you receive at the end of your management training—what you learn while in school is vital to your success as a hotel or restaurant manager. Hotel management programs include instruction in hotel administration, accounting, economics, marketing, housekeeping, food service management and catering, and hotel maintenance engineering.

Restaurant management programs teach nutrition, food planning, and preparation, as well as accounting, business law, management, and computer science. Many programs in restaurant and hotel management combine classroom and laboratory study with internships that provide on-the-job experience (see the section on Internships beginning on page 49). In addition, computer training is included in most programs, because today's hotels and restaurants rely on computers for almost every aspect of business. Technological advances in the industry include Internet-based reservations systems, the creation of Web pages as marketing tools, and the use of the Internet as an outlet for increasing research and education.

Another reason to get formal training is that, in school, you will learn about the wide variety of job opportunities available to you and get a broader vision of what is possible. You might find you don't want to work for a large corporation. You might decide that clubs or educational institutions provide a work atmosphere you would enjoy. The variety of courses available in a good training program will expand your ideas about what a hotel or restaurant manager's job can be.

Formal education will also make available to you vital job search and placement services. The job placement office can be a great source for internships during your schooling, which provide on-the-job training and possibly job offers once completed. Many schools offer courses on how to search for a job, and when your schooling is completed, you may find that a number of local employers actively recruit graduates from your program.

TYPES OF TRAINING PROGRAMS

There are a number of different options when considering the type of education you want and need. If you would like to jump right into the job market, you may be able to receive training while in high school, or on the job after graduation. Or, enroll at a local community college or online institution for a certificate program. If you would like the best chance for a high-paying, rewarding career, consider a bachelor's degree. These and other options are explored in greater detail on the following pages.

High School Hospitality Programs

There are a number of hospitality training programs available to students during high school. Two are offered through the Hospitality Business Alliance (HBA), an educational partnership formed by the National Restaurant Association and the American Hotel & Lodging Association. The programs involve classroom learning as well as mentored internships in actual hotels and restaurants.

The National Restaurant Association Educational Foundation's (NRAEF) program is the HBA/ProStart School-to-Career Initiative. It operates through state restaurant associations, which bring students together with teachers and restaurant and foodservice operators. The NRAEF reported in 2001 that more than 24,000 high school juniors and seniors were studying restaurant and food-service management at 661 schools in 36 states (an increase of 5,000 students from the year before). In addition, 2,800 students were being mentored by industry professionals to complete 400-hour internships.

The two-year ProStart curriculum is designed to teach management skills both in the classroom and in the workplace. Students participate in paid internships, where they are mentored by industry managers. When the program is completed, and students have met academic standards and completed a checklist of competencies, they are awarded the ProStart National Certificate of Achievement that signifies they are qualified to enter the industry workforce. The NRAEF then offers scholarships (see Chapter 3) to certificate holders to further their education. More information may be found on the NRAEF's website, www.nraef.org.

The Educational Institute of the American Hotel and Lodging Association runs a Lodging Management Program (LMP) that provides 11th and 12th grade students with the classroom learning and real-life work experiences needed to take advantage of the lodging industry's employment opportunities. The two-year program is designed to create a foundation to build upon, for students planning an education at a college or university. It also includes internships and mentoring by worksite supervisors. The curriculum of the program is detailed here:

Year One

Unit 1: Overview of Lodging Management
Organization and Structure
Career
Guest Service

Unit 2: The Front Office
The Guest Cycle
Reservations
Check-Out and Settlement
Telecommunications
Registration
The Night Audit

Unit 3: Housekeeping
Housekeeping Management
Guestroom Cleaning
Carpet Construction and Maintenance
Housekeeping Inventory
On-Premises Laundry Management
Safety Management, Chemical, and Security Management

Year Two

Unit 1: Leadership and Management
Leadership and Management
Team Building
Communication Skills
Career Development

Unit 2: Marketing and Sales
Hospitality Marketing and Sales
The Sales Office
Selling is Everyone's Job
The Marketing Plan
Banquet and Meeting Room Sales
Telephone Sales

Unit 3: Food and Beverage Service
Hotels and the Food Service Industry
Dining Room Service
Banquets and Catered Events
The Menu
Casual/Theme Restaurants
Room Service

Source: Educational Institute of the American Hotel and Lodging Association, www.ei-ahla.org.

In addition, the American Hotel and Lodging Association has partnered with Secretary of State Colin Powell's America's Promise Foundation that also offers a "CheckInn" program. This new program entices lodging establishments to "adopt a school," forming a one-on-one relationship in which students interact with staff and management, and learn about careers in hospitality. Check for more information on this new program by searching the Internet with the key word "checkinn."

Another training option available to high school students is Cornell University's Summer Honors Program for High School Sophomores. Cornell's School of Hotel Administration is one of the oldest and best respected programs in the United States. The summer program gives high school students a glimpse of the hotel and restaurant management profession through courses in Managerial Communication and Strategic Perspectives in Hospitality Management. It also offers a preview of a Cornell education; interested students may later apply for admission as candidates for a B.S. degree in nine major areas, or a Master's of Management in Hospitality (M.M.H.). For more information, visit www.hotelschool. cornell.edu/prospective.

Certificate or Diploma Program

These relatively short programs (most are 12 to 24 months) award a certificate or diploma rather than a degree. The course of study might include intensive training in computers, maintenance and housekeeping, and front office management, but fewer general education courses. For example, at Columbia College in Sonora, California, you can earn a certificate in Hotel or Restaurant Management after one year (or less) of study. The courses may be transferable to a degree program if you want to go on with your training. Tuition for the program totals less than $400.00. Here is their 2001 restaurant management curriculum, which is typical of short-term certificate curricula elsewhere:

HPMGT 97—Work Experience
HPMGT 102—Introduction to Hospitality Careers and Human
   Relations
HPMGT 104—Hospitality Laws and Regulations
HPMGT 120—Safety and Sanitation
HPMGT 122—Restaurant Math
HPMGT 126—Nutrition for Chefs
HPMGT 128—Kitchen Management
HPMGT 133A—Intro to Commercial Food Preparation
HPMGT 133B—Commercial Food Preparation
HPMGT 134—Commercial Baking: Beginning
HPMGT 136—Dining Room Service and Management
HPMGT 147—Beverage Management
HPMGT 152—Restaurant Planning

Plus One of the Following:
BUSAD 1A—Principles of Accounting
BUSAD 160—Basic Accounting
BUSAD 161A—Small Business Accounting I
Recommended Optional Course:
HPMGT 148—Introduction to Wines

Source: Columbia College, columbia.yosemite.cc.ca.us

Associate of Applied Science Degree

The associate of applied science degree is a two-year program that involves instruction in business and specific hotel/restaurant topics, as well as basic humanities courses such as English and psychology. It also prepares the student to enter the final two years of a four-year program leading to a bachelor's degree. Middlesex County College in New Jersey offers a degree in Hotel-Motel Management or Restaurant Foodservice Management. The following is the Hotel-Motel Management curriculum. Tuition runs $4,900 for in-county residents, and $9,800 for those residing outside of Middlesex County.

COURSES	CREDITS
ENG 121 English Composition I	3
HRI 101 Intro to Hotel, Restaurant & Institution Management	3
HRI 103 Principles of Food Selection & Preparation	3
HRI 208 Environmental Sanitation in Food Service Operations	3
Mathematics Elective	3–4
Physical/Health Ed Elective	1–3
ACC 108 Accounting Practices for Hotels, Restaurants & Institutions	4
BUS 107 Computer Applications for Business	3
ENG 122 English Composition II	3
HRI 108 Quantity Food Production	3
HRI 110 Supervisory Dev. in the Lodging & Foodservice Industry	3
HRI 201 Hotel-Motel Front Office Operations	3
HRI 206 Merchandising for the Hospitality Industry	3
HRI 217 Supervisory Housekeeping	3

PSY 123 Introductory Psychology	3
Humanities Elective	3
Social Science Elective	3
HRI 203 Volume Food Management & Production	4
HRI 216 Hospitality Property Management	3
HRI Elective	3
General Education Elective	3
Science Elective	3–4
TOTAL CREDITS	66–70

Source: Middlesex County College, www.middlesex.cc.nj.us.

The Bachelor of Arts or Bachelor of Science Degree

This is probably the most common degree for those seeking a position as a manager in a hotel or restaurant. Most schools require that students take a mix of industry-specific courses and those covering general business topics. A bachelor's degree is normally completed in four years, and comprises approximately 120 credits.

If you are worried about the time commitment, check around with the schools you are interested in. Many offer part-time study options, and night and weekend classes so that your education doesn't get in the way of your family or work obligations. If the cost of a four-year degree seems prohibitive, read Chapter 3, which covers the types of financial aid available to students in all fields.

Here are course descriptions from Michigan State University's School of Hospitality Business. Students working toward a bachelor's degree are also required to take courses from other departments, in subjects such as math, science, and the humanities. Tuition at Michigan State is $4,972.50 per year for Michigan residents.

HB 200 (3) Introduction to the Hospitality Industry
Survey of all sectors, segments and disciplines of the hospitality and tourism industries. Topics include the impact of travel and tourism, hospitality trends, and an overview of accounting, marketing, and human resources.

HB 210 (3) Introduction to Casinos
Introduction to casino games of chance, management controls, marketing plans, and the social issues of gaming.

HB 211 (3) Club Operations and Management
Class consists of lectures by the instructor and other club industry specialists as well as individual study and research. Site visits will be arranged to operating city, country, yacht, and athletic clubs. Emphasis will be on functional inter-relationships and Hospitality Management concepts in club settings.

HB 237 (3) Management of Lodging Facilities
Operational departments and logical functions in the operation of various types of lodging properties. Includes planning and control of physical, mechanical, and electrical systems.

HB 265 (3) Quality Food Management
Standards of microbiology, sanitation, nutrition, and other quality issues in food management. Chemical, health, workplace standards that affect staff members and guests. Management of product quality/costs at each control point.

HB 302 (3) Hospitality Managerial Accounting
Principles of managerial accounting applied to hospitality enterprises. Topics include financial statements, forecasting methods, internal control, and accounting ethics.

HB 307 (3) Organizational Behavior in the Hospitality Industry
Human resource management and development of interpersonal skills in the hospitality industry. Focus on managing in a culturally diverse workplace.

HB 320 (3) Casino Operations and Management
Practices and problems associated with casino management, staffing, security, protection of table games, and control.

HB 337 (3) Hospitality Information Systems
Traditional and state-of-the-art technology for gathering, analyzing, storing and communicating information within the hospitality industry.

HB 345 (3) Quality Food Production Systems
Basic organization of food and beverage operations. Product knowledge with particular attention given to purchasing, storing, preparing and production of food products in foodservice operations. Menu development, with focus on product and preparation choices. Recipe management. Laboratory required.

HB 410 (3) Casino Controls and Finance

Gaming regulation of the casino industry, casino cash controls, accounting controls, slot machine controls, financial reporting requirements.

HB 411 (3) Hospitality Beverages

Identification and evaluation of beverages typically served in hospitality establishments with a focus on making quality decisions. Beverages presented will include alcohol (spirits, wines, liqueurs, and beer), coffee, tea, soft drinks, and mineral waters.

HB 415 (3) Total Quality Management in the Hospitality Industry

Continuous quality improvement based on the pioneer work of W. Edwards Deming. Quality planning and control, assessment, customer surveys and feedback, and the cost of quality.

HB 473 (3) Hospitality Industry Research

Strategies and techniques for obtaining, analyzing, evaluating and reporting relevant hospitality research data.

HB 475 (3) Innovations in Hospitality Marketing

Marketing of hospitality industry products and concepts, amid global competition and culturally diverse markets and workforces.

HB 482 (3) Hospitality Managerial Finance

Cash flow determination and management. Strategies for financing hospitality ventures and expansion. Determining the financial viability of proposed and existing operations through traditional and state-of-the-art techniques.

HB 485 (3) Advanced Foodservice Management

Food production management, dining room service, and essentials of alcoholic beverage management. Guest relations and current management topics. Emphasis on foodservice team projects; planning, organizing, production, service, delivery, and evaluation of foodservice events.

HB 489 (3) Policy Issues in Hospitality Management

Complex management problems and issues in the hospitality industry that require policy-making. Focus on decision-making models. Case study analysis, discussion, and written reports.

HB 490 Independent Study in Hospitality Management

Planned research in hospitality management and operations. One, two, or three credits.

HB 491 (3) Current Topics in the Hospitality Industry
Focus on emerging topic(s) and/or issue(s) confronting the hospitality service industry. Provide discussion on topics and issues of importance to the industry.
HB 807 (3) Workforce Management in the Hospitality Industry
Development of effective leadership styles and methods of identifying and solving hospitality workforce problems.
HB 837 (3) Advanced Hospitality Information Systems
Managerial and operational overview of computer systems and network design, implementation and contingency planning in the hospitality industry.
HB 875 (3) Innovative Marketing in the Hospitality Industry
A framework for understanding hospitality marketing in a competitive and global economy.
HB 882 (3) Financial Management in the Hospitality Industry
Interpretation and analysis of hospitality financial statements, budgeting preparation and analysis of variances. Expansion of hospitality businesses through leasing, franchising, management contracts.
HB 885 (3) Seminar in Food and Beverage Systems Management
Foundation information about food and beverage systems' management and operations. Quality food and beverage evaluation.
HB 890 (3) Independent Study in Hospitality Management
Planned research in hospitality management and operations.

Source: Michigan State University School of Hospitality Business, www.bus.msu.edu/shb.

Master's Degree Programs

Most master's degree programs in hotel and restaurant management are geared toward those already working in the field. Therefore, they are primarily offered part-time, or even online, in order to accommodate work schedules. The program at the Conrad N. Hilton College of Hotel and Restaurant Management at the University of Houston offers a Master's in Hotel Management which may be completed online. At Florida State University's Dedman School of Hospitality, part-time students take a mix of management-oriented classes and advanced level classes in hospitality administration, and are awarded a Master of Science in Management with a Major in Hospitality and Tourism. For residents of Florida, the program costs $5,871.60; out-of-state residents are charged $20,529.36. The curriculum is as follows:

HFT 5245—Managing Service Organizations (3 hrs)

HFT 5555—Services Marketing & Research (3 hrs)

HFT 5697—Legal Environment of Hospitality & Tourism Organizations (3 hrs)

HFT 5477—Finance and Cost Control Systems for Hospitality & Tourism Operations (3 hrs)

MAR 5935r—Special Topics in Marketing (3 hrs)

MAN 5935r—HAT Management Project (3 hrs)

MAN 5716—Business Conditions Analysis (3 hrs)

MAN 5245—Organizational Behavior (3 hrs)

FIN 5445—Problems in Financial Management (3 hrs)

MAN 5721—Strategy and Business Policy (3 hrs)

MAR 5935r—Special Topics in Marketing (3 hrs)

MAN 5601—Multinational Business Operations (3 hrs)

Source: Florida State University, www.cob.fsu.edu/grad/hat.

On-the-Job Training

If, after careful consideration, you decide you want to start work without special training, you may be able to learn the skills you need on the job. To bypass formal education, you will need to be certain of the kind of work you want to do, and secure a job in that field with an employer who is willing to train you. Look for larger companies that own many lodging establishments or restaurants, because they are the ones who offer the most comprehensive education to their employees.

The greatest advantage of on-the-job training is expense; you will receive a salary while training, rather than being unemployed and having the expense of training. Be aware that it is advisable—and probably necessary—to get some kind of formal training, because, as discussed earlier, the nature of hospitality management work is changing all the time and you will need to keep abreast of changes in technology.

Distance Education

Distance education—formerly referred to as *correspondence school*—is also an option for training, although it is not usually used as the sole educational experience as it can be with other careers. Because of the hands-on nature of hotel and restaurant management and the need for great people skills, a blend of distance education, classroom learning, and an internship is preferable to employers. For this reason, you won't find many schools offering a degree in your chosen field that can be obtained without an on-campus component.

Distance education differs from what is offered at other schools in that your instruction is given through a variety of delivery systems, rather than the traditional teacher-and-students-in-the-classroom setup. Some rely heavily on the computer, providing Web-based interactive lessons over the Internet, while others allow you to read text and take exams at your own pace. Increasingly, interactive video broadcasts to distant sites are being used. Usually, they are referred to as Web casts or net conferences, and involve your attendance in one location to watch an instructor giving a lesson from another. You have the opportunity to interact with your teacher and other students through the use of video cameras and monitors.

The most attractive feature of distance learning is flexibility; for most of these programs, you can work in your home, at your pace. You need to be highly organized, disciplined, and motivated to succeed in distance education, and some people shy away from it for these same reasons. Find out more about available programs at www.distancelearn.about.com.

If home study seems like the best option for you, use the same criteria spelled out beginning on the following page when choosing a program. Then also consider the type of delivery system used, and determine not only your own familiarity with the technology (if any), but also whether the institution provides student training and technical assistance during the course. Find out how much interaction takes place among teachers and students during courses—are teachers available via phone, e-mail or meeting in-person?

Ask the school for the names of former students whom you can contact for information about their experiences with the school. Get complete information on the course of study and compare it with the curricula of schools you know to be reputable. Make sure that the distance education school you choose is accredited by an organization such as the Distance

Education and Training Council (www.detc.org). The U.S. Department of Education can tell you about other accrediting agencies; contact them at 400 Maryland Avenue, SW, Washington, DC 20202-0498 (800-872-5327), on online at www.ed.gov. Finally, check with the Chamber of Commerce, the Better Business Bureau, or the attorney general's office in the state where the school is headquartered to see if the school has had complaints lodged against it.

CHOOSING A TRAINING PROGRAM

Selecting the training program that will best suit your needs, likes, and goals means making many decisions, including those about the type of school, overall size of the school, location, and quality of programs. Would you prefer large classes held in lecture halls, or smaller classes in which you get to know your teachers? Do you want to go to a local school and live at home, or are you willing to relocate and perhaps live in on-campus housing?

You can explore these options and many others by enlisting the help of an experienced high school guidance counselor or career counselor. Keep asking questions—of yourself and them—until you have the information you need to make your decision. If you are not currently in school, use the online college guides listed in this chapter, and the resources listed in Appendix B at the end of this book, to help you.

To give you even more "insider" information, this book contains interviews with many people in the hospitality industry, and their comments are included throughout the text. You should seek out experienced hotel or restaurant managers, and speak with them about their experiences. Ask where they went to school, what advantages they gained from their education, and what they would do differently if they were starting again.

Which Educational Setting is Right for You?

As mentioned earlier in this chapter, there are six types of programs offered in a variety of settings. By now you probably have a good idea as to the program you are interested in, based on your current level of education and career goals. Read on to explore the types of schools that offer hotel and/or restaurant management programs.

If you are interested in a certificate program, will live at home, and work while getting your education, you might consider a community college. Community colleges are public institutions offering vocational and academic courses both during the day and at night. They cost less than both two- and four-year public and private institutions, and usually require a high school diploma or GED for admission.

You can find out the location of community colleges in your area by contacting your state's Department of Higher Education (listed in Appendix C). Or check the Web through a search engine such as Yahoo.com for community colleges, which are listed by state. Junior colleges are two-year institutions that are usually more expensive than community colleges because they tend to be privately owned. You can earn a two-year degree (Associate of Arts or Associate of Science), which can usually be applied to four-year programs at most colleges and universities. Use the Internet or *Peterson's Two-Year Colleges* guide to help you with your search.

Colleges and universities offer undergraduate (usually four-year) programs in which you can earn a bachelor's or master's degree in a variety of fields. Entrance requirements are more stringent than for community colleges; admissions personnel will expect you to have taken certain classes in high school to meet their admission standards. Your high school GPA (grade point average) and standardized test scores (most often the Scholastic Aptitude Test [SAT]) will be considered. If your high school grades are weak or it has been some time since you were last in school, you might want to consider taking courses at a community college first. You can always apply to the college or university as a transfer student after your academic track record has improved.

Be aware that state or public colleges and universities are generally less expensive to attend than private colleges and universities because they receive state funds to offset their operational costs. Another thing to consider when choosing a college is whether they have placement programs for hotel and restaurant managers. Do they have a relationship with those in the area who hire, in which the employers actively recruit on campus? Attending a school with such a relationship could greatly improve your chances of employment upon graduation.

Online College Guides

Most of these sites offer similar information, including various search methods, the ability to apply to many schools online, financial aid and scholarship information, and online test taking (PSAT, SAT, etc.). Some offer advice in selecting schools, give virtual campus tours, and help you decide what classes to take in high school. It is well worth it to visit several of them.

- **www.collegenet.com**—on the Web since 1995, best for applying to schools online
- **www.collegequest.com**—run by Peterson's, a well-known publisher of college guide books (they can also be found at www.petersons.com)
- **www.collegereview.com**—offers good general information, plus virtual campus tours
- **www.embark.com**—a good general site
- **www.review.com**—a service of The Princeton Review. Plenty of "insider information" on schools, custom searches for schools, pointers on improving standardized test scores
- **www.theadmissionsoffice.com**—answers your questions about the application process, how to improve your chances of getting accepted, when to take tests

Evaluating Your Needs

We have discussed the types of training available and the schools that offer them. Before making a final decision, you will want to consider two more things: Your needs, and the quality of the schools you are interested in. First, make a determination about what you want and need from a training program in terms of:

▶ location
▶ finances
▶ scheduling

Read through the descriptions of these concerns on the following pages, and make notes regarding your position on each of them. You may want to devise a checklist of those items you determine to be "must haves" from the schools you are considering.

Where to Get Your Training

There are excellent training programs offered at schools throughout the country. To select one, you will need to decide where you want to be while getting your education. The best decision from a financial point of view may be to attend school near your home, so you don't incur the added cost of room and board. However, you may wish to attend only the most prestigious, competitive programs in the country, and be willing to relocate in order to attend one of them.

Since there are employment opportunities for hotel and restaurant managers throughout the country and abroad, where you go to school geographically probably won't have much impact on your ability to find a job. However, there are advantages to attending school in the job market in which you will later work. It will allow you to make contacts for future job hunting. Your school may help with job placement locally, and it may employ as teachers people who are in a position to hire hotel and/or restaurant managers. Your instructors can thus be sources of employment later. Networking is discussed in greater detail in Chapter 4, but keep in mind that having friends from school when you are out in the job market can be a big help.

Finances

Costs of the various programs, and the differences in costs between each type of school, have been touched on previously in this chapter. Now, you will need to think more specifically about what you can afford. While there are many sources of funding for your education (check out Chapter 3), and schools do sometimes offer full or partial scholarships, you will still need to spend some money in order to get a quality education.

When evaluating the schools you are interested in, be sure to find out all the costs, not just tuition. You will have to purchase books, which can cost hundreds of dollars over the course of the program (over a thousand dollars if you are considering a bachelor's degree). There may be extra supplies or materials fees for your course of study. If you won't live at home, you will need to pay for room and board—which can total as much as your tuition at some schools. Will you need childcare while attending classes, or have to drive long distances to get to school? Consider those additional costs when calculating how much you will have to spend.

Don't rule out any schools in which you have an interest at this point. Just be sure to gather as much information as you can about real cost of attendance. Read through Chapter 3 to understand all of your options regarding financing your education. Then, you will be prepared to make an informed decision about which program to attend in terms of what you can afford.

Scheduling

When making a choice about training, you should also think about your schedule and the commitments you may already have made. For instance, do you currently have a job you would like to continue working at while you are in school? You will need to find a program that offers classes at times when you are not working. Will an internship interfere with your employment? It might be a good idea to speak with your employer about your plans and goals. He or she may be willing to offer some flexibility.

If you have young children at home, or some other responsibility that requires your energy and time, consider how you will manage both that responsibility and your education. Some schools offer low-cost childcare to their students. Or perhaps another family member or friend could help while you are attending classes or studying. Be sure to think through all of the potential obstacles to your training and seek out ways to overcome them. The schools themselves may be a source of assistance as well, so don't hesitate to ask how other students have managed, or how the school can accommodate you.

Another option is part-time attendance. If you are under financial constraints, you can spread the cost of the program over a greater amount of time. If you have young children at home, need to continue working while getting your education, or have another time constraint, part-time attendance can allow you the flexibility your busy schedule demands. But be aware that while both the financial and time commitments to the program are significantly reduced, it is only for the short term. In total, you will have spent the same, or more, time and money getting your degree or certificate.

When you have considered what you want in terms the type of program, location, costs, and scheduling, you will be able to make a decision about the type of school to attend. Now, you will need to evaluate those schools that meet your criteria in order to find the one that best suits your needs.

Evaluating the Schools

At this point, you should be able to make decisions about the type of program and school you would like to attend, significantly narrowing down the number of schools that you are considering. After consulting the resources in this chapter, make a list of the school or schools offering what you want. Then, for each entry on your list, ask the questions we have outlined here. If you don't have enough information, call the school's admissions director and either ask the questions directly or request more information in the form of school brochures, course descriptions, and other documents. Since many schools have their own websites, you may be able to find your answers on the Internet.

▶ *What are the qualifications of the faculty?*
There should be a balance of faculty members with advanced degrees (M.A., M.B.A., Ph.D., J.D., etc.) and experience in the working world. The faculty should be accessible to students for conferences.

▶ *What is the student-teacher ratio?*
It is important that the student-teacher ratio not be too high. Education suffers if classrooms are too crowded or if a teacher has too many students to accommodate everyone who may wish to schedule a private conference. According to one of the top national accrediting agencies, the Accrediting Council for Independent Colleges and Schools (ACICS), a reasonable student-teacher ratio for skills training is 30 students to one teacher in a lecture setting and 15 students to one teacher in a laboratory or clinical instruction setting. At very good schools the ratio is even better than the ACICS recommends.

▶ *Does the school offer extensive computer training and the latest technology?*
It is a good idea when you are visiting schools—and you should definitely visit the schools you are seriously considering—to ask to see their lab facilities. Part of the accreditation process of a school includes evaluation of its technological facilities, as well as of its library and other instructional resources, so accreditation is a good sign that the school is up to par. However, you will need instruction in the most recent and best computer technology and the latest software designed for use in hotels and restaurants. Check to see if you will receive

instruction in any or all of the following, considered essential at publication time:

AH&MA FRONT OFFICE SIMULATION PROGRAM—provides hands-on exercises in all phases of the guest cycle

"ALLIANTLINK.COM" INTERNET PURCHASING NETWORK—provides a "live" purchasing experience through partnership with Alliant Foodservice

"ALOHA" POINT-OF-SALE SYSTEM—a touch-screen pre-check system for restaurant operations

"COMPUTER CHEF" NUTRITIONAL ANALYSIS—allows the student to analyze the nutritional components of any recipe, and make desired modifications

"COSTGUARD" RESTAURANT MANAGEMENT SOFTWARE—a complete Windows-based back-of-the-house management program

"EBSCO-Host"—online business research database of magazine and newspaper articles

"INNBASKET"—management skills simulation exercise

"INNSYSTEMS 80" PROPERTY MANAGEMENT SOFTWARE—includes reservations, check-in and check-out, accounting, security functions and marketing applications

INTERNET RESOURCES FOR HOSPITALITY MANAGERS—for marketing, reservations, recruiting and decision-making

"MEETING MATRIX" FOR WINDOWS—Computer-Assisted Design (CAD) program for planning meeting and banquet functions

"MENU MAKER"—advanced menu presentation software

"ON COOKING" RECIPE MANAGEMENT—a computerized extension of the Food Fundamentals course textbook

"SCHEDULE MAKER"—for creating, modifying, and analyzing employee schedules

Source: Adapted from Champlain College, www.champlain.edu.

▶ *Is the school accredited?*

It is important that the school you choose be accredited. Accreditation is a tough, complex process and ensures sound educational and ethical business practices at the schools which have achieved this. It is a process schools undergo voluntarily. Some accrediting agencies are national, some regional. The name of the agency proffering accreditation for the school you are interested in will probably be plainly printed on the school's general catalog, or you can obtain the name of the agency by calling the school. In addition, each accrediting agency will send you, free of charge, a directory of the schools it accredits.

If you would like a directory, or have a question about the school you have chosen, you may call the agency that accredits that school, and its personnel will help you. See Accrediting Agencies in Appendix C for names, addresses, and phone numbers. Keep in mind that if you choose a school that is not accredited, you will not be able to get financial aid through any government programs.

The International Council on Hotel, Restaurant, and Institutional Education (CHRIE) recommends two accrediting bodies: The Accreditation Commission for Programs in Hospitality Administration™ (ACPHA™), which accredits hospitality administration programs at the baccalaureate level, and the Commission for Accreditation of Hospitality Management Programs (CAHM) which accredits hospitality management programs at the associate degree or equivalent level. Check Appendix C to see if your school of choice is accredited by these agencies.

Both Commissions' membership includes voting representatives from accredited hospitality programs, hospitality industry professionals, international programs, the public at large, and ex-officio representatives from CHRIE. The Commissions have set up accrediting standards that represent those characteristics determined to be essential in order for program objectives to be achieved. The standards consider the resources of school (inputs), as well as the outcome (including student placement rate, titled output). The standards for both Commissions cover the following areas:

- mission and objectives
- evaluation and planning
- administration and governance
- curriculum
- faculty/instructional staff
- student services, activities, and resources

► *What is the school's job placement rate for graduates?*

A school's job placement rate for graduates is extremely important. Usually schools offer placement services free of charge, often for the working lifetime of their graduates. All accredited private schools must place a percentage (determined to be "reasonable" by the accrediting agency) of their students in order to maintain accreditation. Many good schools boast placement rates of 90% or more, such as Champlain College in Burlington, Vermont, which has a current placement rate of 97%.

A good job placement office will offer:

- resume writing and cover-letter writing assistance
- job leads—full time, part time, permanent, and temporary
- networking opportunities with employers in the area (often as a part of an internship while the student is still in school)
- seminars on job hunting
- career counseling and simulated interviews
- lifetime placement assistance for graduates

► *Does the school have a good internship program?*

The value of internships is discussed later in the chapter, but it is important to consider the quality of a school's internship program before deciding on a hospitality management program. The variety of internships makes schools located near a large city especially attractive. As part of the accreditation process, schools must monitor the internship program to ensure the students are introduced to meaningful work, not simply relegated to filing or other menial tasks. A good internship will give you many advantages when you are ready to find your first job.

ADMISSION REQUIREMENTS

Depending upon the program you are interested in, admission requirements may be as simple as having a high school diploma (or GED), and filling out an application. Or, you may need high scores on the SAT or ACT, and to have graduated within the top 10% of your high school class. Community colleges offering certificate programs and associate degrees are typically the easiest to get into. Many have an "open admission" policy, meaning that they will accommodate anyone interested in their programs. Others may ask that you take the SAT or ACT if you are applying for a degree, but may accept modest scores.

Colleges and universities require more of their applicants. You will have to fill out a lengthy application form (many schools share a common one), and you may be given the option of completing and submitting it online. While some schools are more competitive than others, all will look at your grade point average (GPA) from high school and your test scores (SAT or ACT), so you will have to arrange to have these sent directly to the schools you are applying to. Your high school transcript may be compared with those of other applicants as the college looks to see who has taken more rigorous courses. You may be required to write a personal essay which highlights not only your writing skills, but also your ability to sell your personality, your activities, and your ideas.

More competitive schools receive far more applications than they have slots in their freshman class, so they can be highly selective. Larger schools that admit many more students each year are less selective when offering admission. The following are a few schools offering bachelor's degrees in hotel and or restaurant management, along with some of their admission requirements.

Utah Valley State College in Orem offers a Bachelor of Science in hospitality management with a specialization area in food and beverage management. It accepts 100% of its applicants. The average ACT score is 20, and just 19% of its freshman class ranked in the top 25% of their high school class. In contrast, Georgia State University in Atlanta, which offers a Bachelor of Science degree in hospitality management, accepts just 59% of those who apply. The average SAT score of their applicants is 1035, and 10% of their incoming freshmen were in the top 10% of their high school class.

James Madison University in Virginia also confers Bachelor of Science degrees in hospitality management, and accepts 64% of those who apply. 78% of their freshman class was in the top 25% of their high school class. At Bowling Green State University's College of Business Administration in Ohio, a student must first apply to the university, and gain acceptance as a pre-business administration major. The school accepts 88% of those who apply, with an average ACT score of 22. However, to get a degree in restaurant or hospitality management, students must take eight pre-professional core courses, earning a minimum grade point average of 2.25. Then, they can apply to the Bachelor of Science in Business Administration program; admission is competitive and based on academic performance.

To get an idea of how competitive the schools you are interested in are, check out the online college guides listed on page 41. Many have databases of thousands of schools which you can search and compare results. They contain information about acceptance rates, selectivity, and other criteria.

MAKING THE MOST OF YOUR TRAINING PROGRAM

Once you have chosen a program of study, completed the application process, and have been accepted, there are a number of ways to guarantee that the time, effort, and money you spend on the program are maximized.

Internships

An internship is one way to get job experience before you enter the "real" workforce. Almost every training program for hotel and restaurant managers includes internships as part of its curriculum. Although there are basically three types, all internships are designed as learning experiences, giving the intern exposure to an actual working environment. Internships can be one of the following:

1. paid—the intern receives a salary for his/her work
2. college—the intern is a student, and usually receives college credit for his/her work
3. summer—the intern is likely to be a student, who may or may not receive college credit

College internships may be the easiest to find, because your school will place you, or help place you, in one. They have relationships with the restaurants and hotels that use interns and place students with them year after year. Those who offer internships may also look to hire students when they complete their courses of study. For a college internship, you may also have to attend a class with other interns, or prepare a journal detailing your work experience, or write a paper about it.

Michigan State University's School of Hospitality Business requires students to accept two paid internships equaling 800 hours of on-the-job learning during the undergraduate years. This requirement, easily arranged with on-campus support from the Student and Industry Resource Center, provides not only important opportunities for professional and educational growth, but pays immediate dividends for potential job seekers. Employers frequently cite the internship program as their best means for pre-selecting future hires.

You may also get an internship at a resort or other vacation destination, either through your school or by applying directly. For instance, Walt Disney World offers paid internships for students enrolled in hotel and restaurant management degree programs (for more information, log onto their website: www.wdcollegeprogram.com). Champlain College in Burlington, Vermont offers its students internships at a variety of settings, such as nearby Bolton Valley Ski Resort and Wyndham Sugar Bay Beach Club in St. Thomas.

In addition, larger corporations in the hospitality industry offer paid internships to college students. Some even recruit students on campus for their programs. The Marriott International Internship provides an opportunity to work in finance and accounting, banquets/catering, culinary arts, front office, housekeeping, human resources, restaurant/room service/lounge, or sales. Top internees may also be selected to attend a three-day Student Leadership Summit, a conference that stresses problem solving skills, team building tactics, and the sharing of real life work experiences.

If your school does not provide help in finding internships, or does not offer credit for them, you can find one for yourself (such as Disney World's, mentioned earlier). There are a number of ways in which you can uncover an opportunity, either during the summer, a semester off, or once you have graduated. If your school hires those working in the hospitality industry to teach some courses, consider enrolling in them. You may be able to make a contact or contacts that could lead to an internship. The Internet is also a good source of information. There, you can learn about all stages of the internship experience, including identifying learning objectives, managing "office politics," self-monitoring and documentation, and how to use the internship to land a permanent job. Three sites that offer listings of internships available nationwide are www.internships.com, www.internjobs.com, and www.vault.com.

The following books are also excellent resources:

▶ *America's Top Internships, 2000 Edition.* Mark Oldman (New York: Princeton Review).
▶ *Internship Success.* Marianne Ehrlich Green (New York: McGraw Hill, 1998).
▶ *Peterson's 2000 Internships* (Lawrenceville, NJ: Peterson's Guides).
▶ *The Yale Daily News Guide to Internships 2000.* John Anselmi (New York: Kaplan).

When you locate specific internship opportunities, some of the questions you will want to ask include:

▶ How many work hours are required to receive credit?
▶ If applicable, how much does the internship pay?
▶ Will you be graded for your work? If so, by a college professor or the person you work under at the company you intern for?
▶ Do you have to arrange your own internship with the company or work through your school?
▶ Does the internship program at your school also require you to attend classes, write a paper, or make a presentation to a faculty member in order to receive credit?
▶ What will your responsibilities be on a day-to-day basis?
▶ Who, within the company, will you be working for?
▶ Will the internship provide real-world work experience that is directly related to your chosen field?
▶ Will your participation in the internship provide you with networking opportunities?

Once you land an internship, consider it an audition for ultimately obtaining a full-time job. Always act professionally, ask questions, follow directions, display plenty of enthusiasm, volunteer to take on additional responsibilities, meet deadlines, and work closely with your boss/supervisor. Upon graduating, make sure to highlight your internship work on your resume.

Having an internship on your resume will make you stand out to a recruiter for a number of reasons. First, it shows that you are already familiar with a professional environment and know what is expected of you. Second, you have proven yourself through performance to a potential employer (you may want to get a letter of recommendation and include it with your resume). Third, you have shown that, after evaluating the realities of the job, you are still eager to pursue it. For all of the reasons detailed here, it makes great sense for you to get an internship. Claire Andrews, a director of programs at Casco Bay College in Portland, Maine, notes:

> It's really important to me that the students do get out there, whether it's through a part-time job or through an internship, to get practical experience. Otherwise, waving that certificate means nothing.

Getting the Most Out of Your Classes

Successful completion of your education depends upon a number of things, including your performance during internships, scoring well on tests, writing great papers, and even getting along well with the faculty and fellow students. The classroom is the setting in which most of these factors come together. You will attend class almost every day, providing plenty of opportunity to learn and prove yourself. There are three things you must do in order to get the most out of your classes:

1. Complete all assignments before class.
2. Take good notes while completing assignments and during class. An outline style of note-taking works best to organize information and make studying easier.

3. Ask questions about anything you don't understand as topics are introduced—do not wait until exam time.

By completing your assignments on schedule, you will be able to get the most out of your time spent in the classroom. Most likely, your instructor will base his or her lesson on assigned reading. If you come to class prepared, the lecture will not only make more sense, but will build upon what you learned in the reading(s). You will also be able to participate in discussions, which may count toward your final grade. If there was anything in the assignment that you didn't understand, you will have the chance to ask for clarification.

If you never learned how to take good notes, you will need to acquire this skill while in your training program. Check out the resources in Appendix B for help, but also be on the lookout for a classmate who appears to be a great note-taker. If he or she is willing to share, you can learn by example. Many successful students find that they can reinforce the material covered by copying over their notes. Don't wait too long to do this, though, especially if your notes are sloppy and difficult to read. Read through what you have written, and decide if the notes could be better organized. Then, copy them back into your notebook. The "cleaned up" version of your notes will help when it comes time to study for exams.

You may also want to highlight material in the margins of your notes that didn't make sense to you. During your next class, you can ask questions and get the clarification you need. Make sure you understand everything that is presented to you as quickly as possible. If you wait until exam time, it may be difficult under such pressure to take in large amounts of new information.

Preparing for Exams

As mentioned, good preparation throughout the semester will make studying for exams much easier. Studying for an exam should be about going over material you already know—not reading assignments for the first time or trying to learn a semester's worth of data in a day or two. Begin preparing for an exam by reading over your notes. Look for any areas that you indicated you didn't understand at the time and make sure you understand them now. If you don't, talk to your instructor or do some extra reading until the concept is clear.

Then, try making an outline of the class. Organize the material in a way that makes sense to you, using Roman numerals for the main topics, capitalized letters for subtopics, and Arabic numerals to break down subtopics further. For more information, check the study guides suggested in Appendix B.

Most important, on the evening before the exam, relax, eat a good dinner, and get a good night's sleep. In the morning, eat a good breakfast (and lunch, if it is an afternoon test). Try to take a walk or get some other light exercise, if you have time before the exam. During the exam, stay calm and have faith in yourself and your abilities.

Your Social Life

During your education, there will be interesting people sitting next to you in class and teaching your classes. These people have experiences and knowledge that can be a benefit to you. You can help each other by studying together and creating an information loop that keeps everyone informed—not only about what is happening in class, but throughout the school as well. Forging friendships with teachers and students can make the transition from student to hotel or restaurant manager easier as well. After graduation, these are the people who may be able to help you get your first job. They may also be your colleagues throughout your career.

If the program you are in offers social events, take advantage of them as often as you can. And make it a point early in your academic career to get to know those in your counseling and placement offices. These people know the answers to almost all your questions and can be an invaluable resource.

Your management training is the first, essential step on the road to your chosen career. Don't view it simply as something to get through, as an ordeal you must overcome before you can begin work and start your real life. School is the time to learn as much about the profession and yourself as you possibly can. Along the way, you will make friends and contacts—sometimes they will be the same person—who will be equally valuable to you as you finish school and embark on your career.

THE INSIDE TRACK

Who: Cherie Chandler
What: Assistant Manager, Capri Restaurante
Where: Englewood, New Jersey

INSIDER'S STORY

I work as a dining room manager in a family-run Italian restaurant in northern New Jersey, just outside of New York City. The owner is a business associate of my uncle, so I guess you could say I have an "in."

Some people think that my job is nothing more than a glorified hostess position. It looks like a really fun job, greeting customers and taking down names, but most people don't even realize the hard work that goes into it. That's probably why a good, competent dining room manager's job looks so easy. I've worked as a waitress in the past, which is a tough job, and I understand what the wait staff needs from me, in addition to what my responsibilities are to the customers, so I think that makes my evenings at work go smoothly.

In the dining room, you do a little bit of everything, from taking reservations, to making sure that all the servers are present and presentable, to checking the tables and bus stations for cleanliness, and of course greeting and seating customers. Also, I make sure that the cash registers are set up, and that everyone is aware of the nightly specials. The first hour is usually quiet, then we spring into action when the after-work crowd starts coming in. You need to know which servers are busy, which need another table, and know how to stagger seating the guests so that the servers aren't overwhelmed. Seeing to the wait staff's needs is a consuming part of every night. Also, you need to recognize regulars and VIPs and seat them at the best tables to ensure that they keep coming back. As a matter of fact, that brings up the most important function—making every guest feel welcome, comfortable, and satisfied with their dining experience. People spend a lot of money on dinner here—it's one of those restaurants you go to for special occasions—so it's my job to make sure that they have a great evening.

I went to community college here in Jersey and got an Associate's degree in hospitality. I enjoyed my program, and I learned a lot about customer service and handling guests, but I think that the hands-on experience I've had in restaurants over the years is what has really prepared me for the nightly challenges that occur on the job.

I know that restaurant work isn't for everyone—there are a lot of late nights and your work schedule tends to be the opposite of your friends and family. I love the evening hours because they really suit my lifestyle. My fiancé is a musician, so he works at night, too. I enjoy getting dressed up to greet the customers at work, then I'm usually all set to meet up with the band after the restaurant closes. I sleep late—just like in college. I have my days free to shop or visit family and go to the gym most every afternoon.

My advice for anyone considering the restaurant business is to remember that it's a fun, fast-paced environment, but at the end of the day, it's also a lot of hard work. You need to take your role seriously so that others' work goes smoothly. If you mess up, your mistake can throw off the entire shift. You're on your feet, interacting with customers the whole time, so an even temper and patience is important. You can't get cranky and still manage to greet guests with a genuine smile, so you must learn to roll with whatever the evening brings. There will always be customers who don't like waiting for a table, then, inevitably, they are seated at a table too close to the kitchen. They tend to want to move to the table right next to where you or the hostess just sat a party of six. You can anticipate what happens next; the waitress gets mad at you because you "double sat" her, and now her rhythm is off. She's upset until you fix it, so you get the drinks from the bar and give her a break, only to turn around and find a hungry mob scene at the door. The next time you look at your watch, it's midnight. You haven't eaten, your feet hurt, and the table in the corner looks like they will never go home. You wait. You get their coats, and breathe a sigh of relief when they are out the door. You cash out the wait staff, reconcile the accounts, check the dining room set up for the next day and leave to unwind, then rest up for the next night . . . you live off the energy that only the restaurant can provide.

CHAPTER three

FINANCIAL AID—DISCOVERING THE POSSIBILITIES

IN CHAPTER 2 you learned how to find and succeed in the right training program for you. This chapter explains some of the many different types of financial aid available, gives you information on what financial records you will need to gather to apply for financial aid, and helps you through the process of applying for financial aid. (A sample financial aid form is included in Appendix D.) At the end of the chapter are listed many more resources that can help you find the aid you need.

YOU HAVE decided on a career as a hotel or restaurant manager and you've chosen a training program. Now, you need a plan to finance your training. Perhaps you or your family have been saving for your education, and you've got the money to pay your way. Or maybe your employer offers some money to help its employees attend school. However, if you are like most students, you don't have enough to cover the cost of the training program you'd like to attend. Be assured that it is likely that you can qualify for some sort of financial aid, even if you plan to attend school only part-time.

Because there are many types of financial aid, and the millions of dollars given away or loaned are available through so many sources, the process of finding funding for your education can seem confusing. Read through this chapter carefully, and check out the many resources, including the websites and publications listed in Appendix B. You will have a better understanding of where to look for financial aid, what you can qualify for, and how and when to apply.

Also take advantage of the financial aid office at the school you've chosen, or your guidance counselor if you're still in high school. These professionals can offer plenty of information, and can help to guide you through the process. If you're not in school, and haven't chosen a program yet, check the Internet. It's probably the best source for up-to-the-minute information, and almost all of it is free. There are a number of great sites at which you can fill out questionnaires with information about yourself and receive lists of scholarships and other forms of financial aid for which you may qualify. You can also apply for some types of federal and state aid online—you can even complete the Free Application for Federal Student Aid (FAFSA), the basic form that determines federal and state financial aid eligibility, online if you choose (see a sample FAFSA in Appendix D).

SOME MYTHS ABOUT FINANCIAL AID

The subject of financial aid is often misunderstood. Here are some of the most common myths:

Myth #1: All the red tape involved in finding sources and applying for financial aid is too confusing for me.

Fact: The whole financial aid process is a set of steps that are ordered and logical. Besides, several sources of help are available. To start, read this chapter carefully to get a helpful overview of the entire process and tips on how to get the most financial aid. Then, use one or more of the resources listed within this chapter and in the appendices for additional help. If you believe you will be able to cope with your training program, you will be able to cope with looking for the money to finance it—especially if you take the process one step at a time in an organized manner.

Myth #2: For most students, financial aid just means getting a loan and going into heavy debt, which isn't worth it, or working while in school, which will lead to burnout and poor grades.

Fact: Both the federal government and individual schools award grants and scholarships which a student doesn't have to pay back. It is also possible to get a combination of scholarships and loans. It's worth taking out a loan if it means attending the program you really want to attend, rather than settling for your second choice or not pursuing a career in your chosen field at all. As for working while in school, it's true that it is a challenge to hold down a full-time or even part-time job while in school. However, a small amount of work-study employment (10–12 hours per week) has been shown to actually improve academic performance, because it teaches students important time-management skills.

Myth #3: I can't understand the financial aid process because of all the unfamiliar terms and strange acronyms that are used.

Fact: While you will encounter an amazing number of acronyms and some unfamiliar terms while applying for federal financial aid, you can refer to the acronym list and glossary at the end of this chapter for quick definitions and clear explanations of the commonly used terms and acronyms.

Myth #4: Financial aid is for students attending academic colleges or universities. I'm going to a vocational training program so I won't qualify.

Fact: This is a myth that far too many people believe. The truth is, there is considerable general financial aid for which vocational students qualify. There are also grants and scholarships specifically designed for students in vocational programs. The financial aid you get may be less than that for longer, full-time programs, but it can still help you pay for a portion of your training program.

Myth #5: My family makes too much money (or I make too much money), so I shouldn't bother to apply for financial aid.

Fact: The formula used to calculate financial aid eligibility is complex and takes more into account than just your or your family's income. Also, some forms of financial aid—such as a PLUS Loan or an unsubsidized Stafford Loan—are available regardless of calculated financial need. The only way to be certain NOT to get financial aid is to NOT apply; don't shortchange yourself by not applying, even if you think you won't be eligible.

TYPES OF FINANCIAL AID

There are three categories of financial aid:

1. Grants and scholarships—aid that you don't have to pay back
2. Work-Study—aid that you earn by working
3. Loans—aid that you have to pay back

Each of these types of financial aid will be examined in greater detail, so you will be able to determine which one(s) to apply for, and when and how to apply. Note that grants and scholarships are available on four levels: Federal, state, school, and private.

Grants

Grants are normally awarded based on financial need. Even if you believe you won't be eligible based on your own or your family's income, don't skip this section. There are some grants awarded for academic performance and other criteria. The two most common grants are the Federal Pell Grant and Federal Supplemental Educational Opportunity Grant (FSEOG).

Federal Pell Grants

Federal Pell Grants are based on financial need and are awarded only to undergraduate students who have not yet earned a bachelor's or professional degree. For many students, Pell Grants provide a foundation of financial aid to which other aid may be added. For the year 2001–2002, the maximum award was $3,750.00. You can receive only one Pell Grant in an award year, and you may not receive Pell Grant funds for more than one school at a time.

How much you get will depend not only on your Expected Family Contribution (EFC), but also on your cost of attendance, whether you're a full-time or part-time student, and whether you attend school for a full academic year or less. You can qualify for a Pell Grant even if you are only enrolled part-time in a training program. You should also be aware that some private- and school-based sources of financial aid will not consider your eligibility if you haven't first applied for a Pell Grant.

Federal Supplemental Educational Opportunity Grants (FSEOG)

Priority consideration for FSEOG funds is given to students receiving Pell Grants because the FSEOG program is based on exceptional financial need. An FSEOG is similar to a Pell Grant in that it doesn't need to be paid back.

If you are eligible, you can receive between $100 and $4,000 a year in FSEOG funds depending on when you apply, your level of need, and the funding level of the school you're attending. The FSEOG differs from the Pell Grant in that it is not guaranteed that every needy student will receive one because each school is only allocated a certain amount of FSEOG funds by the federal government to distribute among all eligible students. To have the best chances of getting this grant, apply for financial aid as early as you can after January 1 of the year in which you plan to attend school.

State Grants

State grants are generally specific to the state in which you or which your parents reside. If you and your parents live in the state in which you will attend school, you've got only one place to check. However, if you will attend school in another state, or your parents live in another state, be sure to check your eligibility with your state grant agency. Not all states allow their state grants to be used at out-of-state schools. There is a list of state agencies included in Appendix C with telephone numbers and websites, so you can easily find out if there is a grant for which you can apply.

Scholarships

Scholarships are often awarded for academic merit or for special character-istics (for example, ethnic heritage, personal interests, sports, parents' career, college major, geographic location) rather than financial need. As with grants, you do not pay your award money back. Scholarships may be offered from federal, state, school, and private sources.

The best way to find scholarship money is to use one of the free search tools available on the Internet. After entering the appropriate information about yourself, a search takes place which ends with a list of those prizes for which you are eligible. Try www.fastasp.org, which bills itself as the world's largest and oldest private sector scholarship database. A couple of other good sites for conducting searches are www.college-scholarships.com and www.gripvision.com. If you don't have easy access to the Internet, or want to expand your search, your high school guidance counselors or college financial aid officers also have plenty of information about available scholar-ship money. Also, check out your local library.

To find private sources of aid, spend a few hours in the library looking at scholarship and fellowship books or consider a reasonably priced (under $30) scholarship search service. See the Resources section at the end of this chapter to find contact information for search services and scholarship book titles.

Also, contact some or all of the professional associations for the program you're interested in attending; some offer scholarships, while others offer information about where to find scholarships. If you're currently employed, find out if your employer has scholarship funds available. If you're a depend-ent student, ask your parents and other relatives to check with groups or organizations they belong to as well as their employers to see if they have scholarship programs or contests. Investigate these popular sources of scholarship money:

▶ religious organizations
▶ fraternal organizations
▶ clubs (such as Rotary, Kiwanis, American Legion, Grange, or 4-H)

▶ athletic clubs

▶ veterans' groups (such as the Veterans of Foreign Wars)

▶ ethnic group associations

▶ unions

▶ local chambers of commerce

If you already know which school you will attend, check with a financial aid administrator (FAA) in the financial aid office to find out if you qualify for any school-based scholarships or other aid. Many schools offer merit-based aid for students with a high school GPA of a certain level or with a certain level of SAT scores in order to attract more students to their school. Check with your program's academic department to see if they maintain a bulletin board or other method of posting available scholarships.

While you are looking for sources of scholarships, continue to enhance your chances of winning one by participating in extracurricular events and volunteer activities. You should also obtain references from people who know you well and are leaders in the community, so you can submit their names and/or letters with your scholarship applications. Make a list of any awards you've received in the past or other honors that you could list on your scholarship application. There are thousands of scholarships awarded to students planning careers in hotel or restaurant management. To find more sources, search the Internet using terms such as "restaurant manager" and "scholarship." Following are some samples of those available:

Academic Scholarship

Offered by the National Restaurant Association's Educational Foundation

Amount of Award: $2000.00

Who's eligible: high school seniors

To be considered for this scholarship, applicants must have:

▨ A minimum grade point average of 2.75 on a 4.0 scale (or equivalent) verified by a transcript from each high school attended. (Unofficial transcripts will be accepted; report cards will not.)

▨ A letter of acceptance indicating that you have enrolled in an accredited restaurant or foodservice related post-secondary program as a full-time or substantial part-time (minimum 9 credit hours) student where you plan to remain for a minimum of two terms.

- A minimum of 250 hours of restaurant- or foodservice-related work experience verified by copies of paycheck stubs or letter(s) from employer(s) stipulating number of hours worked.
- A letter of recommendation on letterhead from a current/previous employer in the restaurant or foodservice industry.

ProStart® National Certificate of Achievement Scholarship

Offered by the National Restaurant Association Educational Foundation

Who's eligible: Students who have received the ProStart National Certificate of Achievement by participating in the HBA/ProStart School-to-Career Initiative.

To be considered for this scholarship, applicants must have:

- A copy of the National Restaurant Association Educational Foundation's ProStart National Certificate of Achievement.
- A letter of acceptance indicating that you have enrolled in an accredited culinary and/or restaurant/foodservice management related post-secondary program as a full-time or substantial part-time (minimum 9 credit hours) student where you plan to remain for a minimum of two terms.
- A Cumulative Grade Point Average (GPA). Please include it on application.

Academic Scholarship for Undergraduate College Students

Offered by the National Restaurant Association Educational Foundation

Amount of award: $2000.00

To be considered for this scholarship, applicants must:

- Be currently enrolled in a college or university on a full-time or substantial part-time basis where you have completed at least one term with a minimum grade point average of 2.75 on a 4.0 scale (or equivalent).
- Have a copy of college curriculum as described in your college catalog with the number of credit hours detailed. (Please do not include the entire catalog—only the information as it pertains to your major.)
- Provide a transcript from each college attended (unofficial transcripts will be accepted; report cards will not). Transcripts sent separately are required to be postmarked by deadlines established for the application or the application will be disqualified.

- Have proof of restaurant or foodservice-related work experience with a minimum of 750 hours verified by copies of paycheck stubs or letter(s) from employer(s) stipulating number of hours worked. (W-2s are NOT valid proof of hours worked.)
- Have a letter of recommendation on letterhead from a current/previous employer in the restaurant or foodservice industry.

The Network of Executive Women in Hospitality, Inc.'s Arizona Chapter Scholarship

Award amount: $2000.00

Who's Eligible: Female students at Arizona State University entering their junior year

Applicants must have:

- completed half the requirements for a degree or certification program in which enrolled
- real financial need
- a 3.0 GPA
- a career objective in the Hospitality Industry (i.e., Hotel/Restaurant Management, Culinary, Food Service, Architecture, Design, etc.)

For more information, email the NEWH at office@newh.org.

The Arthur J. Packard Memorial Scholarship Competition

Offered by the American Hotel and Lodging Association

Amount of award: $5000.00 plus trip to New York for presentation of award for first place; $3000.00 for second place; $2000.00 for third place

Who's Eligible: Lodging management students enrolled in AH&LA affiliated four-year programs

Each university nominates the one student most qualified according to the criteria to compete in the national competition. The deadline date for receipt of applications is April 1. Students should inquire in their dean's office for consideration of the nomination and application.

American Express Scholarship Program

Amount of award: $500 to $2000

Who's eligible: Lodging employees, working a minimum of 20 hours a week at American Hotel & Lodging Association (AH&LA) member properties, and their dependents. If you or your parents are working at a hotel, ask your general manager if your property is a member of AH&LA and the state hotel association.

The program offers two types of scholarships:

- Academic Scholarships: Provides financial support to students enrolled in an accredited undergraduate academic program leading to a degree in hospitality management. Scholarship amounts can range between $500 and $2,000 depending on enrollment status. The applicant does not have to be attending an AH&LA affiliated school.

- Professional Development Scholarships: Provides financial support to students enrolled in distance learning courses or professional certifications courses offered through the Educational Institute (EI) of AH&LA. Applicants must be enrolled or intend to enroll in the Educational Institute program to qualify. AH&LA makes scholarship payment directly to EI on the recipient's behalf.

Call EI at 800-390-8399 for enrollment information. Individuals can apply directly to AH&LA for scholarship consideration. The deadline for the academic scholarships is May 1 and quarterly for EI scholarships.

A program benefiting mainly middle-class students is the Hope Scholarship Credit. Eligible taxpayers may claim a federal income tax credit for tuition and fees up to a maximum of $1,500 per student (the amount is scheduled to be reindexed for inflation after 2002). The credit applies only to the first two years of postsecondary education, and students must be enrolled at least half-time in a program leading to a degree or a certificate. To find out more about the Hope Scholarship Credit, log onto www.sfas. com.

For the Lifetime Learning Credit, eligible taxpayers may claim a federal income tax credit for tuition and fees up to a maximum of $1,000 per student through the year 2002. After the year 2002, eligible taxpayers may claim a credit for tuition and fees up to a maximum of $2,000 per student (unlike the Hope Scholarship Credit, this amount will not be reindexed for inflation after 2002). The Lifetime Learning Credit is not limited to the first two years of postsecondary education; students in any year can be eligible, and there is no minimum enrollment requirement. For more information about the Lifetime Learning Credit, log onto www.sfas.com.

The National Merit Scholarship Corporation offers about 5,000 students scholarship money each year based solely on academic performance in high school. If you are a high school senior with excellent grades and high scores on tests such as the ACT or SAT, ask your guidance counselor for details about this scholarship.

You may also be eligible to receive a scholarship from your state or school. Check with the higher education department of the relevant state or states (listed in Appendix C), or the financial aid office of the school you will attend.

Work-Study Programs

When applying to a college or university, you can indicate that you are interested in a work-study program. Their student employment office will have the most information about how to earn money while getting your education. Work options include the following:

▶ on- or off-campus
▶ part-time or almost full-time
▶ school- or nationally-based
▶ in some cases, in your program of study (to gain experience) or not (just to pay the bills)
▶ for money to repay student loans or to go directly toward educational expenses

If you're interested in school-based employment, the student employment office can give you details about the types of jobs offered (which can range from giving tours of the campus to prospective students to working in the cafeteria to helping other students in a student services office) and how much they pay.

You should also investigate the Federal Work-Study (FWS) program, which can be applied for on the Free Application for Federal Student Aid (FAFSA). The FWS program provides jobs for undergraduate and graduate students with financial need, allowing them to earn money to help pay education expenses. It encourages community service work and provides hands-on experience related to your course of study, when available. The amount of the FWS award depends on:

▶ when you apply (apply early!)
▶ your level of need
▶ the FWS funds available at your particular school

FWS salaries are the current federal minimum wage or higher, depending on the type of work and skills required. As an undergraduate, you will be paid by the hour (a graduate student may receive a salary), and you will receive the money directly from your school; you cannot be paid by commission or fee. The awards are not transferable from year to year, and not all schools have work-study programs in every area of study.

An advantage of working under the FWS program is that your earnings are exempt from FICA taxes if you are enrolled full-time and are working less than half-time. You will be assigned a job on-campus, in a private non-profit organization, or a public agency that offers a public service. The total wages you earn in each year cannot exceed your total FWS award for that year and you cannot work more than 20 hours per week. Your financial aid administrator (FAA) or the direct employer must consider your class schedule and your academic progress before assigning your job.

For more information about National Work-Study programs, visit the Corporation for National Service website (www.cns.gov) and/or contact:

▶ **National Civilian Community Corps (NCCC)**—This AmeriCorps program is an 11-month residential national service program intended for 18–24-year-olds. Participants receive $4,725.00 for college tuition or to help repay education loan debt. Contact: National Civilian Community Corps, 1100 Vermont Avenue NW, Washington, DC 20525, 800-94-ACORPS.

▶ **Volunteers in Service to America (VISTA)**—VISTA is a part of ACTION, the deferral domestic volunteer agency. This program offers numerous benefits to college graduates with outstanding student loans. Contact: VISTA, Washington, DC 20525, 800-424-8867.

If you are already working in the field in which you intend to go to school, your employer may help you pay for job-related courses. Check with your employer for details.

Student Loans

Although scholarships, grants, and work-study programs can help to offset the costs of higher education, they usually don't give you enough money to entirely pay your way. Most students who can't afford to pay for their entire education rely at least in part on student loans. The largest single source of these loans—and for all money for students—is the federal government. However, you can also find loan money from your state, school, and/or private sources.

Try these sites for information about U.S. government programs:

www.fedmoney.org
This site explains everything from the application process (you can actually download the applications you will need), eligibility requirements, and the different types of loans available.

www.finaid.org
Here, you can find a calculator for figuring out how much money your education will cost (and how much you will need to borrow), get instructions for filling out the necessary forms, and even information on the various types of military aid (which will be detailed in the next chapter).

www.ed.gov/offices/OSFAP/students
This is the Federal Student Financial Aid Homepage. The FAFSA (Free Application for Federal Student Aid) can be filled out and submitted online. You can find a sample FAFSA in Appendix D, to help familiarize yourself with its format.

www.students.gov
This bills itself as the "student gateway to the U.S. government" and is run as a cooperative effort under the leadership of the Department of

Education. You can find information about financial aid, community service, military service, career development, and much more.

You can also get excellent detailed information about different federal sources of education funding by sending away for a copy of the U.S. Department of Education's publication, *The Student Guide*. Write to: Federal Student Aid Information Center, P.O. Box 84, Washington, DC 20044, or call 800-4FED-AID.

Listed below are some of the most popular federal loan programs:

Federal Perkins Loans

A Perkins Loan has the lowest interest (currently, it's 5%) of any loan available for both undergraduate and graduate students, and is offered to students with exceptional financial need. You repay your school, which lends the money to you with government funds.

Depending on when you apply, your level of need, and the funding level of the school, you can borrow up to $4,000 for each year of undergraduate study. The total amount you can borrow as an undergraduate is $20,000 if you have completed two years of undergraduate study; otherwise, you can borrow a maximum of $8,000.

The school pays you directly by check or credits your tuition account. You have nine months after you graduate (provided you were continuously enrolled at least half-time) to begin repayment, with up to ten years to pay off the entire loan.

PLUS Loans (Parent Loan for Undergraduate Students)

PLUS Loans enable parents with good credit histories to borrow money to pay the education expenses of a child who is a dependent undergraduate student enrolled at least half-time. Your parents must submit the completed forms to your school.

To be eligible, your parents will be required to pass a credit check. If they don't pass, they might still be able to receive a loan if they can show that extenuating circumstances exist or if someone who is able to pass the credit check agrees to co-sign the loan. Your parents must also meet citizenship requirements and not be in default on any federal student loans of their own.

The yearly limit on a PLUS Loan is equal to your cost of attendance minus any other financial aid you receive. For instance, if your cost of attendance is $10,000 and you receive $5,000 in other financial aid, your parents could borrow up to, but no more than, $5,000. The interest rate varies, but is not to exceed 9% over the life of the loan. Your parents must begin repayment while you're still in school. There is no grace period.

Federal Stafford Loans

Stafford Loans are low-interest loans that are given to students who attend school at least half-time. The lender is the U.S. Department of Education for schools that participate in the Direct Lending program and a bank or credit union for schools that do not participate in the Direct Lending program. Stafford Loans fall into one of two categories:

Subsidized loans are awarded on the basis of financial need. You will not be charged any interest before you begin repayment or during authorized periods of deferment. The federal government subsidizes the interest during these periods.

Unsubsidized loans are not awarded on the basis of financial need. You will be charged interest from the time the loan is disbursed until it is paid in full. If you allow the interest to accumulate, it will be capitalized—that is, the interest will be added to the principal amount of your loan, and additional interest will be based upon the higher amount. This will increase the amount you have to repay.

There are many borrowing limit categories to these loans, depending on whether you get an unsubsidized or subsidized loan, which year in school you're enrolled, how long your program of study is, and if you're independent or dependent. You can have both kinds of Stafford Loans at the same time, but the total amount of money loaned at any given time cannot exceed $23,000 for a dependent undergraduate student and $46,000 as an independent undergraduate student (of which not more than $23,000 can be in subsidized Stafford Loans). The interest rate varies, but will never exceed 8.25%. An origination fee for a Stafford Loan is approximately 3% or 4% of the loan, and the fee will be deducted from each loan disbursement you receive. There is a six-month grace period after graduation before you must start repaying the loan.

State Loans

Loan money is also available from state governments. In Appendix C, you will find a list of the agencies responsible for giving out such loans, with websites and e-mail addresses when available. Remember that you may be able to qualify for a state loan based on your residency, your parents' residency, or the location of the school you're attending.

Alternative Loans

Alternative loans are loans either you, you and a co-borrower, or your parent can take out based on credit; usually the maximum you can borrow is for the cost of education minus all other financial aid received. Interest rates vary but are generally linked to the prime rate. Some of the many lenders who offer these types of loans are listed in the resources section at the end of this chapter. You can also ask your local bank for help or search the Internet for "alternative loans for students."

Questions to Ask Before You Take Out a Loan

In order to get the facts regarding the loan you're about to take out, ask the following questions:

1. What is the interest rate and how often is the interest capitalized? Your college's financial aid administrator (FAA) will be able to tell you this.

2. What fees will be charged? Government loans generally have an origination fee that goes to the federal government to help offset its costs, and a guarantee fee, which goes to a guaranty agency for insuring the loan. Both are deducted from the amount given to you.

3. Will I have to make any payments while still in school? It depends on the type of loan, but often you won't; depending on the type of loan, the government may even pay the interest for you while you're in school.

4. What is the grace period—the period after my schooling ends—during which no payment is required? Is the grace period long enough, realistically, for you to find a job and get on your feet? (A six-month grace period is common.)

5. When will my first payment be due and approximately how much will it be? You can get a good preview of the repayment process from the answer to this question.

6. Who exactly will hold my loan? To whom will I be sending payments? Who should I contact with questions or inform of changes in my situation? Your loan may be sold by the original lender to a secondary market institution, in which case you will be notified as to the contact information for your new lender.

7. Will I have the right to prepay the loan, without penalty, at any time? Some loan programs allow prepayment with no penalty but others do not.

8. Will deferments and forbearances be possible if I am temporarily unable to make payments? You need to find out how to apply for a deferment or forbearance if you need it.

9. Will the loan be canceled ("forgiven") if I become totally and permanently disabled, or if I die? This is always a good option to have on any loan you take out.

APPLYING FOR FINANCIAL AID

Now that you're aware of the types and sources of aid available, you will want to begin applying as soon as possible. You've heard about the Free Application for Federal Student Aid (FAFSA) many times in this chapter already, and should now have an idea of its importance. This is the form used by federal and state governments, as well as schools and private funding sources, to determine your eligibility for grants, scholarships, and loans. The easiest way to get a copy is to log onto www.ed.gov/offices/OSFAP/ students, where you can find help in completing the FAFSA, and then submit the form electronically when you are finished. You can also get a copy by calling 1-800-4FED-AID, or by stopping by your public library or your school's financial aid office. Be sure to get an original form, because photocopies of federal forms are not accepted.

The second step of the process is to create a financial aid calendar. Using any standard calendar, write in all of the application deadlines for each step of the financial aid process. This way, all of your vital information will be in one location, so you can see at a glance what needs to be done and when it's due. Start this calendar by writing in the date you requested your FAFSA. Then, mark down when you received it and when you sent in the completed form (or just the date you filled the form out online if you chose to complete the FAFSA electronically). Add important dates and deadlines for any other applications you need to complete for school-based or private aid as you progress though the financial aid process. Using and maintaining a calendar will help the whole financial aid process run more smoothly and give you peace of mind that the important dates are not forgotten.

When to Apply

Apply for financial aid as soon as possible after January 1 of the year in which you want to enroll in school. For example, if you want to begin school in the fall of 2002, then you should apply for financial aid as soon as possible after January 1, 2002. It is easier to complete the FAFSA after you have completed your tax return, so you may want to consider filing your taxes as early as possible as well. Do not sign, date, or send your application before January 1 of the year for which you are seeking aid. If you apply by mail, send your completed application in the envelope that came with the original application. The envelope is already addressed, and using it will make sure your application reaches the correct address.

Many students lose out on thousands of dollars in grants and loans because they file too late. Don't be one of them. Pay close attention to dates and deadlines.

After you mail in your completed FAFSA, your application will be processed in approximately four weeks. (If you file electronically, this time estimate is considerably shorter.) Then, you will receive a Student Aid Report (SAR) in the mail. The SAR will disclose your Expected Family Contribution (EFC), the number used to determine your eligibility for federal student aid. Each school you list on the application may also receive your application information if the school is set up to receive it electronically.

You must reapply for financial aid every year. However, after your first year, you will receive a Student Aid Report (SAR) in the mail before the application deadline. If no corrections need to be made, you can just sign it and send it in.

Getting Your Forms Filed

Follow these three simple steps if you are not completing and submitting the FAFSA online:

1. Get an original Federal Application for Federal Student Aid (FAFSA). Remember to pick up an original copy of this form, as photocopies are not accepted.

2. Fill out the entire FAFSA as completely as possible. Make an appointment with a financial aid counselor if you need help. Read the forms completely, and don't skip any relevant portions or forget to sign the form (or forget to have your parents sign, if required).

3. Return the FAFSA long before the deadline date. Financial aid counselors warn that many students don't file the forms before the deadline and lose out on available aid. Don't be one of those students!

Financial Need

Financial aid from many of the programs discussed in this chapter is awarded on the basis of need (the exceptions include unsubsidized Stafford, PLUS, consolidation loans, and some scholarships and grants). When you apply for federal student aid by completing the FAFSA, the information you report is used in a formula established by the United States Congress. The formula determines your Expected Family Contribution (EFC), an amount you and your family are expected to contribute toward your education. If your EFC is below a certain amount, you will be eligible for a Pell Grant, assuming you meet all other eligibility requirements.

There is no maximum EFC that defines eligibility for the other financial aid options. Instead, your EFC is used in an equation to determine your financial needs. Eligibility is a very complicated matter, but it can be simplified to the following equation: your contribution + your parents' contribution = expected family contribution (EFC). Student expense budget/cost of attendance (COA) – EFC = your financial need.

The need analysis service or federal processor looks at the following if you are a dependent student:

▶ Family assets, including savings, stocks and bonds, real estate investments, business/farm ownership, and trusts
▶ Parents' ages and need for retirement income
▶ Number of children and other dependents in the family household
▶ Number of family members in college
▶ Cost of attendance, also called student expense budget; includes tuition and fees, books and supplies, room and board (living with parents, on campus, or off campus), transportation, personal expenses, and special expenses such as childcare

A financial aid administrator calculates your cost of attendance and subtracts the amount you and your family are expected to contribute toward that cost. If there's anything left over, you're considered to have financial need.

Are You Considered Dependent or Independent?

Federal policy uses strict and specific criteria to make this designation, and that criteria applies to all applicants for federal student aid equally. A dependent student is expected to have parental contribution to school expenses, and an independent student is not.

You're an independent student if at least one of the following applies to you:

▶ you were born before January 1, 1979 (for the 2002–2003 school year)
▶ you're married (even if you're separated)
▶ you have legal dependents other than a spouse who get more than half of their support from you and will continue to get that support during the award year
▶ you're an orphan or ward of the court (or were a ward of the court until age 18)
▶ you're a graduate or professional student

▶ you're a veteran of the U.S. Armed Forces—formerly engaged in active service in the U.S. Army, Navy, Air Force, Marines, or Coast Guard or as a cadet or midshipman at one of the service academies—released under a condition other than dishonorable. (ROTC students, members of the National Guard, and most reservists are not considered veterans, nor are cadets and midshipmen still enrolled in one of the military service academies.)

If you live with your parents, and if they claimed you as a dependent on their last tax return, then your need will be based on your parents' income. You do not qualify for independent status just because your parents have decided to not claim you as an exemption on their tax return (this used to be the case but is no longer) or do not want to provide financial support for your college education.

Students are classified as *dependent* or *independent* because federal student aid programs are based on the idea that students (and their parents or spouse, if applicable) have the primary responsibility for paying for their postsecondary education. If your family situation is unusually complex and you believe it affects your dependency status, speak to a financial aid counselor at the school you plan to attend as soon as possible. In extremely limited circumstances a financial aid office can make a professional judgment to change a student's dependency status, but this requires a great deal of documentation from the student and is not done on a regular basis. The financial aid office's decision on dependency status is *final* and cannot be appealed to the U.S. Department of Education.

Gathering Financial Records

Your financial need for most grants and loans depends on your financial situation. Now that you've determined if you are considered a dependent or independent student, you will know whose financial records you need to gather for this step of the process. If you are a dependent student, then you must gather not only your own financial records, but also those of your parents because you must report their income and assets as well as your own when you complete the FAFSA. If you are an independent student, then you need to gather only your own financial records (and those of your spouse if you're married). Gather your tax records from the year prior to the one in which you are applying. For example, if you apply for the fall of 2002, you will use your tax records from 2001.

Filling Out the FAFSA

To help you fill out the FAFSA, gather the following documents:

- U.S. Income Tax Returns (IRS Form 1040, 1040A, or 1040EZ) for the year that just ended and W-2 and 1099 forms
- records of untaxed income, such as Social Security benefits, AFDC or ADC, child support, welfare, pensions, military subsistence allowances, and veterans' benefits
- current bank statements and mortgage information
- medical and dental expenses for the past year that weren't covered by health insurance
- business and/or farm records
- records of investments such as stocks, bonds, and mutual funds, as well as bank certificates of deposit (CDs) and recent statements from money market accounts
- Social Security number(s)

Even if you do not complete your federal income tax return until March or April, you should not wait to file your FAFSA until your tax returns are filed with the IRS. Instead, use estimated income information and submit the FAFSA, as noted earlier, just as soon as possible after January 1. Be as accurate as possible, knowing that you can correct estimates later.

Maximizing Your Eligibility for Loans and Scholarships

Loans and scholarships are often awarded based on an individual's eligibility. Depending on the type of loan or scholarship you pursue, the eligibility requirements will be different. EStudentLoan.com (www.estudentloan.com) offers the following tips and strategies for improving your eligibility when applying for loans and/or scholarships:

1. Save money in the parent's name, not the student's name.
2. Pay off consumer debt, such as credit card and auto loan balances.
3. Parents considering going back to school should do so at the same time as their children. Often, the more family members in school simultaneously, the more aid will be available to each.
4. Spend student assets and income first, before other assets and income.
5. If you believe that your family's financial circumstances are unusual, make an appointment with the financial aid administrator at your school to review your case. Sometimes the school will be able to adjust your financial aid package to compensate.
6. Minimize capital gains.
7. Do not withdraw money from your retirement fund to pay for school. If you must use this money, borrow from your retirement fund.
8. Minimize educational debt.
9. Ask grandparents to wait until the grandchild graduates before giving them money to help with their education.
10. Trust funds are generally ineffective at sheltering money from the need analysis process, and can backfire on you.
11. If you have a second home, and you need a home equity loan, take the equity loan on the second home and pay off the mortgage on the primary home.

GENERAL GUIDELINES FOR LOANS

Before you commit yourself to any loans, be sure to keep in mind that they need to be repaid. Estimate realistically how much you will earn when you leave school, remembering that you will have other monthly obligations such as housing, food, and transportation expenses.

Once You're in School

Once you have your loan (or loans) and you're attending classes, don't forget about the responsibility of your loan. Keep a file of information on your loan that includes copies of all your loan documents and related correspondence, along with a record of all your payments. Open and read all your mail about your education loan(s).

Remember also that you are obligated by law to notify both your financial aid administrator (FAA) and the holder or servicer of your loan if there is a change in your:

- ▶ name
- ▶ address
- ▶ enrollment status (dropping to less than half-time means that you will have to begin payment six months later)
- ▶ anticipated graduation date

After You Leave School

After graduation, you must begin repaying your student loan immediately, or begin after a grace period. For example, if you have a Stafford Loan you will be provided with a six-month grace period before your first payment is due; other types of loans have grace periods as well. If you haven't been out in the working world before, your loan repayment begins your credit history. If you make payments on time, you will build up a good credit rating, and credit will be easier for you to obtain for other things. Get off to a good start, so you don't run the risk of going into default. If you default (or refuse to pay back your loan) any number of the following things could happen to you as a result. You may:

- ▶ have trouble getting any kind of credit in the future
- ▶ no longer qualify for federal or state educational financial aid
- ▶ have holds placed on your college records
- ▶ have your wages garnished
- ▶ have future federal income tax refunds taken
- ▶ have your assets seized

To avoid the negative consequences of going into default in your loan, be sure to do the following:

▶ Open and read all mail you receive about your education loans immediately.

▶ Make scheduled payments on time; since interest is calculated daily,
delays can be costly.

▶ Contact your servicer immediately if you can't make payments on time;
he or she may be able to get you into a graduated or income-sensitive/
income contingent repayment plan or work with you to arrange a
deferment or forbearance.

There are a few circumstances under which you won't have to repay your
loan. If you become permanently and totally disabled, you probably will not
have to (providing the disability did not exist prior to your obtaining the aid)
repay your loan. Likewise, if you die, if your school closes permanently in
the middle of the term, or if you are erroneously certified for aid by the
financial aid office you will probably also not have to repay your loan.
However, if you're simply disappointed in your program of study or don't
get the job you wanted after graduation, you are not relieved of your obli-
gation.

Loan Repayment

When it comes time to repay your loan, you will make payments to your
original lender, to a secondary market institution to which your lender has
sold your loan, or to a loan servicing specialist acting as its agent to collect
payments. At the beginning of the process, try to choose the lender who
offers you the best benefits (for example, a lender who lets you pay electronically, offers lower interest rates to those who consistently pay on time,
or who has a toll-free number to call 24 hours a day, 7 days a week). Ask the
financial aid administrator at your college to direct you to such lenders.

Be sure to check out your repayment options before borrowing. Lenders
are required to offer repayment plans that will make it easier to pay back
your loans. Your repayment options may include:

▶ *Standard repayment*: Full principal and interest payments due each
month throughout your loan term. You will pay the least amount of

interest using the standard repayment plan, but your monthly payments may seem high when you're just out of school.

▶ *Graduated repayment*: Interest-only or partial interest monthly payments due early in repayment. Payment amounts increase thereafter. Some lenders offer interest-only or partial interest repayment options, which provide the lowest initial monthly payments available.

▶ *Income-based repayment*: Monthly payments are based on a percentage of your monthly income.

▶ *Consolidation loan*: Allows the borrower to consolidate several types of federal student loans with various repayment schedules into one loan. This loan is designed to help student or parent borrowers simplify their loan repayments. The interest rate on a consolidation loan may be lower than what you're currently paying on one or more of your loans. The phone number for loan consolidation at the William D. Ford Direct Loan Program is 800-557-7392. Financial aid administrators recommend that you do not consolidate a Perkins Loan with any other loans since the interest on a Perkins Loan is already the lowest available. Loan consolidation is not available from all lenders.

▶ *Prepayment*: Paying more than is required on your loan each month or in a lump sum is allowed for all federally sponsored loans at any time during the life of the loan without penalty. Prepayment will reduce the total cost of your loan.

It's quite possible—in fact likely—that while you're still in school your Federal Family Education Loan Program (FFELP) loan will be sold to a secondary market institution such as Sallie Mae. You will be notified of the sale by letter, and you need not worry if this happens—your loan terms and conditions will remain exactly the same or they may even improve. Indeed, the sale may give you repayment options and benefits that you would not have had otherwise. Your payments after you finish school, and your requests for information should be directed to the new loan holder.

If you receive any interest-bearing student loans, you will have to attend exit counseling after graduation, where the loan lenders or financial aid office personnel will tell you the total amount of debt and work out a payment schedule with you to determine the amount and dates of repayment. Many loans do not become due until at least six to nine months after you graduate, giving you a grace period. For example, you do not have to begin paying on the Perkins Loan until nine months after you graduate. This grace period is to give you time to find a good job and start earning money. However, during this time, you may have to pay the interest on your loan.

If for some reason you remain unemployed when your payments become due, you may receive an unemployment deferment for a certain length of time. For many loans, you will have a maximum repayment period of ten years (excluding periods of deferment and forbearance).

THE MOST FREQUENTLY ASKED QUESTIONS ABOUT FINANCIAL AID

Here are answers to some of the most frequently asked questions about student financial aid:

1. *I probably don't qualify for aid—should I apply for it anyway?*
   Yes. Many students and families mistakenly think they don't qualify for aid and fail to apply. Remember that there are some sources of aid that are not based on need. The FAFSA form is free—there's no good reason for not applying.

2. *Do I have to be a U.S. citizen to qualify for financial aid?*
   Students (and parents, for PLUS Loans) must be U.S. citizens or eligible noncitizens to receive federal and state financial aid. Eligible noncitizens are U.S. nationals or U.S. permanent nonresidents (with "green cards"), as well as nonresidents in certain special categories. If you don't know whether you qualify, speak to a financial aid counselor as soon as possible.

3. *Do I have to register with the Selective Service before I can receive financial aid?*
   Male students who are U.S. citizens or eligible noncitizens must register with the Selective Service by the appropriate deadline in order to receive federal financial aid. Call the Selective Service at 847-688-6888 if you have questions about registration.

4. *Do I need to be admitted at a particular university before I can apply for financial aid?*

   No. You can apply for financial aid any time after January 1. However, to get the funds, you must be admitted and enrolled in school.

5. *Do I have to reapply for financial aid every year?*

   Yes, and if your financial circumstances change, you may get either more or less aid. After your first year you will receive a Renewal Application which contains preprinted information from the previous year's FAFSA. Renewal of your aid also depends on your making satisfactory progress toward a degree and achieving a minimum GPA.

6. *Are my parents responsible for my educational loans?*

   No. You and you alone are responsible, unless they endorse or co-sign your loan. Parents are, however, responsible for federal PLUS Loans. If your parents (or grandparents or uncle or distant cousins) want to help pay off your loan, you can have your billing statements sent to their address.

7. *If I take a leave of absence from school, do I have to start repaying my loans?*

   Not immediately, but you will after the grace period. Generally, though, if you use your grace period up during your leave, you will have to begin repayment immediately after graduation, unless you apply for an extension of the grace period before it's used up.

8. *If I get assistance from another source, should I report it to the student financial aid office?*

   Yes—and, unfortunately, your aid amount will possibly be lowered accordingly. But you will get into trouble later on if you don't report it.

9. *Are federal work-study earnings taxable?*

   Yes, you must pay federal and state income tax, although you may be exempt from FICA taxes if you are enrolled full time and work less than 20 hours a week.

10. *My parents are separated or divorced. Which parent is responsible for filling out the FAFSA?*

    If your parents are separated or divorced, the custodial parent is responsible for filling out the FAFSA. The custodial parent is the parent with whom you lived the most during the past 12 months. Note that this is not necessarily the same as the parent who has legal custody. The question of which parent must fill out the FAFSA becomes complicated in many situations, so you should take your particular circumstance to the student financial aid office for help.

FINANCIAL AID CHECKLIST

_____ Explore your options as soon as possible once you've decided to begin a training program.

_____ Find out what your school requires and what financial aid they offer.

_____ Complete and mail the FAFSA as soon as possible after January 1.

_____ Complete and mail other applications by the deadlines.

_____ Return all requested documentation promptly to your financial aid office.

_____ Carefully read all letters and notices from the school, the federal student aid processor, the need analysis service, and private scholarship organizations. Note whether financial aid will be sent before or after you are notified about admission, and how exactly you will receive the money.

_____ Gather loan application information and forms from your school or college financial aid office. You must forward the completed loan application to your financial aid office. Don't forget to sign the loan application.

_____ Report any changes in your financial resources or expenses to your financial aid office so they can adjust your award accordingly.

_____ Re-apply each year.

FINANCIAL AID ACRONYMS KEY

COA	Cost of Attendance (also known as COE, Cost of Education)
CWS	College Work-Study
EFC	Expected Family Contribution
EFT	Electronic Funds Transfer
ESAR	Electronic Student Aid Report
ETS	Educational Testing Service
FAA	Financial Aid Administrator
FAF	Financial Aid Form
FAFSA	Free Application for Federal Student Aid
FAO	Financial Aid Office/Financial Aid Officer

FDSLP	Federal Direct Student Loan Program
FFELP	Federal Family Education Loan Program
FSEOG	Federal Supplemental Educational Opportunity Grant
FWS	Federal Work-Study
PC	Parent Contribution
PLUS	Parent Loan for Undergraduate Students
SAP	Satisfactory Academic Progress
SC	Student Contribution
USED	U.S. Department of Education

FINANCIAL AID TERMS—CLEARLY DEFINED

accrued interest—interest that accumulates on the unpaid principal balance of your loan

capitalization of interest—addition of accrued interest to the principal balance of your loan that increases both your total debt and monthly payments

default (you won't need this one, right?)—failure to repay your education loan

deferment—a period when a borrower, who meets certain criteria, may suspend loan payments

delinquency (you won't need this one, either!)—failure to make payments when due

disbursement—loan funds issued by the lender

forbearance—temporary adjustment to repayment schedule for cases of financial hardship

grace period—specified period of time after you graduate or leave school during which you need not make payments

holder—the institution that currently owns your loan

in-school grace, and **deferment interest subsidy**—interest the federal government pays for borrowers on some loans while the borrower is in school, during authorized deferments, and during grace periods

interest-only payment—a payment that covers only interest owed on the loan and none of the principal balance

interest—cost you pay to borrow money

lender (originator)—puts up the money when you take out a loan; most lenders are financial institutions, but some state agencies and schools make loans too

origination fee—fee, deducted from the principal, which is paid to the federal government to offset its cost of the subsidy to borrowers under certain loan programs

principal—amount you borrow, which may increase as a result of capitalization of interest, and the amount on which you pay interest

promissory note—contract between you and the lender that includes all the terms and conditions under which you promise to repay your loan

secondary markets—institutions that buy student loans from originating lenders, thus providing lenders with funds to make new loans

servicer—organization that administers and collects your loan; may be either the holder of your loan or an agent acting on behalf of the holder

subsidized Stafford Loans—loans based on financial need; the government pays the interest on a subsidized Stafford Loan for borrowers while they are in school and during specified deferment periods

unsubsidized Stafford Loans—loans available to borrowers, regardless of family income; unsubsidized Stafford Loan borrowers are responsible for the interest during in-school, deferment periods, and repayment

FINANCIAL AID RESOURCES

In addition to the sources listed throughout this chapter, these are additional resources that may be used to obtain more information about financial aid.

Telephone Numbers

Federal Student Aid Information Center (U. S. Department of Education)
    Hotline   800-4FED-AID
                                                  (800-433-3243)
    TDD Number for Hearing-Impaired   800-730-8913

For suspicion of fraud or abuse of federal aid	800-MIS-USED (800-647-8733)
Selective Service	847-688-6888
Immigration and Naturalization (INS)	415-705-4205
Internal Revenue Service (IRS)	800-829-1040
Social Security Administration	800-772-1213
National Merit Scholarship Corporation	708-866-5100
Sallie Mae's college AnswerSM Service	800-222-7183
Career College Association	202-336-6828
ACT: American College Testing program (about forms submitted to the need analysis servicer)	916-361-0656
College Scholarship Service (CSS)	609-771-7725; TDD 609-883-7051
Need Access/Need Analysis Service	800-282-1550
FAFSA on the Web Processing/ Software Problems	800-801-0576

Websites

www.ed.gov/prog_info/SFAStudentGuide
The Student Guide is a free informative brochure about financial aid and is available on-line at the Department of Education's Web address listed here.

www.ed.gov\prog_info\SFA\FAFSA
This site offers students help in completing the FAFSA.

www.ed.gov/offices/OPE/t4_codes
This site offers a list of Title IV school codes that you may need to complete the FAFSA.

www.ed.gov/offices/OPE/express
This site enables you to fill out and submit the FAFSA on line. You will need to print out, sign, and send in the release and signature pages.

www.career.org

This is the website of the Career College Association (CCA). It offers a limited number of scholarships for attendance at private proprietary schools. You can also contact CCA at 750 First Street, NE, Suite 900, Washington, DC 20002-4242.

www.salliemae.com

This is the website for Sallie Mae that contains information about loan programs.

www.teri.org

This is the website of The Educational Resource Institute (TERI), which offers alternative loans to students and parents.

www.nelliemae.com

This is the website for Nellie Mae; it contains information about alternative loans as well as federal loans for students and parents.

www.key.com

This is Key Bank's website, which has information on alternative loans for parents and students.

www.educaid.com

This is the website for Educaid, which offers both federal and alternative loans to students and parents.

Software Programs

Cash for Class

Tel: 800-205-9581

Fax: 714-673-9039

Redheads Software, Inc.

3334 East Coast Highway #216

Corona del Mar, CA 92625

E-mail: cashclass@aol.com

C-LECT Financial Aid Module

Chronicle Guidance Publications

P. O. Box 1190

Moravia, NY 13118-1190

Tel: 800-622-7284 or 315-497-0330

Fax: 315-497-3359

Peterson's Award Search

Peterson's

P.O. Box 2123

Princeton, NJ 08543-2123

Tel: 800-338-3282 or 609-243-9111

E-mail: custsvc@petersons.com

Pinnacle Peak Solutions (Scholarships 101)

Pinnacle Peak Solutions

7735 East Windrose Drive

Scottsdale, AZ 85260

Tel: 800-762-7101 or 602-951-9377

Fax: 602-948-7603

TP Software—Student Financial Aid Search Software

TP Software

P.O. Box 532

Bonita, CA 91908-0532

Tel: 800-791-7791 or 619-496-8673

E-mail: mail@tpsoftware.com

Books and Pamphlets

The Student Guide

Published by the U.S. Department of Education, this is the handbook about federal aid programs. To get a printed copy, call 1-800-4FED-AID.

Looking for Student Aid

Published by the U.S. Department of Education, this is an overview of sources of information about financial aid. To get a printed copy, call 1-800-4FED-AID.

How Can I Receive Financial Aid for College?
Published from the Parent Brochures ACCESS ERIC website. Order a printed copy by calling 800-LET-ERIC or write to ACCESS ERIC, Research Blvd-MS 5F, Rockville, MD 20850-3172.

Cassidy, David J. *The Scholarship Book 2002: The Complete Guide to Private-Sector Scholarships, Fellowships, Grants, and Loans for the Undergraduate* (Englewood Cliffs, NJ: Prentice Hall, 2001).

Chany, Kalman A. and Geoff Martz. *Student Advantage Guide to Paying for College 1997 Edition.* (New York: Random House, The Princeton Review, 1997.)

College Costs & Financial Aid Handbook, 18th ed. (New York: The College Entrance Examination Board, 1998).

Cook, Melissa L. *College Student's Handbook to Financial Assistance and Planning* (Traverse City, MI: Moonbeam Publications, Inc., 1991).

Davis, Kristen. *Financing College: How to Use Savings, Financial Aid, Scholarships, and Loans to Afford the School of Your Choice* (Washington, DC: Random House, 1996).

Hern, Davis and Joyce Lain Kennedy. *College Financial Aid for Dummies* (Foster City, CA: IDG Books Worldwide, 1999).

Peterson's Scholarships, Grants and Prizes 2002 (Lawrenceville, NJ: Peterson's, 2001).

Ragins, Marianne. *Winning Scholarships for College: An Insider's Guide* (New York: Henry Holt & Company, 1994).

Scholarships, Grants & Prizes: Guide to College Financial Aid from Private Sources (Princeton, NJ: Peterson's, 1998).

Schwartz, John. *College Scholarships and Financial Aid* (New York: Simon & Schuster, Macmillan, 1995).

Schlacter, Gail and R. David Weber. *Scholarships 2000* (New York: Kaplan, 1999).

Other Related Financial Aid Books

Annual Register of Grant Support (Chicago, IL: Marquis, annual).
A's and B's of Academic Scholarships (Alexandria, VA: Octameron, annual).
Chronicle Student Aid Annual (Moravia, NY: Chronicle Guidance, annual).

College Blue Book. Scholarships, Fellowships, Grants and Loans (New York: Macmillan, annual).

College Financial Aid Annual (Englewood Cliffs, NJ: Prentice Hall, annual).

Directory of Financial Aids for Minorities (San Carlos, CA: Reference Service Press, biennial).

Directory of Financial Aids for Women (San Carlos, CA: Reference Service Press, biennial).

Financial Aids for Higher Education (Dubuque, IA: Wm. C. Brown, biennial).

Financial Aid for the Disabled and their Families (San Carlos, CA: Reference Service Press, biennial).

Leider, Robert and Ann. *Don't Miss Out: the Ambitious Student's Guide to Financial Aid* (Alexandria, VA: Octameron, annual).

Paying Less for College (Lawrenceville, NJ: Peterson's, annual).

THE INSIDE TRACK

Who:　　　　Richard Short
What:　　　　Food and Beverage Director
Where:　　　Hotel Bradly,
　　　　　　　　Portland, Oregon

INSIDER'S STORY

Growing up in the business, I always knew that I would have a career in the hotel industry. When my sister and I were young, we traveled with our parents setting up high-rise, luxury hotels all over the country. I saw them built literally from the ground up, and I knew that I wanted to be one of the "suits" involved in the strategic planning and operations.

I went to college for hotel and restaurant management, which was more difficult than I had anticipated. I focused on business administration, and figured that my dad's franchise would hire me right away as a manager. My dad, however, had other plans. I was impatient, but he understood the value of learning the business from the ground up, just as he had done in his day. I started at the bottom—as an assistant catering manager at a mid-sized hotel chain. Anxious to move up and get on with my career, I channeled my energy and enthusiasm into overhauling the special events program, like weddings and banquets. Before I worked at this chain, it wasn't known in the city as an optimum place for a reception, but I'm proud to say that now they have a competitive package to offer a bride-to-be or a corporate events coordinator.

After two years, I got hired at a four-star hotel in Portland as a food and beverage manager. After six months, the director left on maternity leave, and I took on her responsibilities, mostly extra back-end stuff, like spreadsheets and managing vendor accounts. When she decided not to come back, I was given the title officially. I'm very happy in this busy and varied position, but I know that I'm gaining experience by the day that will be necessary for years to come in this business.

In hindsight, I have to admit that my dad was right—nothing beats experience. I really understand the needs of my subordinates from having been there, actually having once executed their work. I hope to get hired as a manager in the next year. I'm ready for the challenges ahead, and I know what to look for when hiring staff. If you're heading out into the job market, make sure you know what the job entails. Get the most out of your internship, and don't be afraid to get in there and provide service, even if it's not your job function. If a bartender calls in sick, and you're the manager on duty, get behind the bar and serve the patrons or bring up a couple cases of beer from the storage area. Remember, it's all about service and teamwork, and pitching in will get you noticed.

CHAPTER four

FINDING YOUR FIRST JOB

IN THIS CHAPTER you will be walked through the job search process. The many ways to locate a future employer once your hotel or restaurant management training is completed (including some tips on how you may find a job while still in school) will be explained in detail. You will learn how to conduct your job search through networking, researching, using classified ads, reading industry publications, utilizing online resources, visiting job fairs, and contacting job hotlines. Knowing how to find the best employment opportunities is the first step in the job search process.

NOW THAT you have finished, or nearly finished, the education you need to become a hotel or restaurant manager, you are ready to find employment in your chosen field. The job market outlook is great, according to the U.S. Department of Labor. In their *Occupational Outlook Handbook, 2000-01*, the Bureau of Labor Statistics reports that there are over 76,000 hotel managers and half a million restaurant and food service managers currently employed in the United States.

Employment of restaurant and food service managers is expected to increase 10–20% through 2008. While no changes are expected in the employment numbers of hotel managers during the same period, there will be plenty of job openings, due to a high turnover rate, and the retirement or job transfer of those already in the field. The greatest opportunities will be for those who hold two- or four-year degrees in hotel or restaurant management.

The job search process can be time consuming and stressful. But by reading this chapter, you will give yourself an advantage. You will learn how to set goals and formulate career and job objectives. Then you will take an organized approach to the whole procedure by setting deadlines and staying on top of the details. You will also learn how to find and utilize the best resources available to you, including the Internet, your school's career placement office, and networking contacts.

WHAT KIND OF JOB DO YOU REALLY WANT?

A "good job" means something different to everyone. In order to work at one that is right for you, you will first need to decide what you are looking for. Formulating your job objective should be the first step in the job search process. Perhaps your goal is to someday be general manager of a corporation that owns thousands of restaurants. Or maybe you would like to begin managing small hotels, and eventually buy and run your own inn. You might envision yourself as the food service manager at a resort in a warm climate. Or, perhaps you are not sure what type of job you are looking for.

If that is the case, before you begin your job search, take the time to decide on long-term and short-term career goals. Picture yourself in a fulfilling job next week, next year, and five years from now. Are you thinking in terms of one job, or several, moving up the corporate ladder? While you are exploring your needs and wants, write them down. Use two or three columns, for short and long term planning. Keep in mind that your goals should:

▶ describe in detail what you want to accomplish
▶ be measurable, formulated in terms that can clearly be evaluated (for instance, "by next year, I will be employed at a 500-room hotel")
▶ be challenging, taking energy and discipline to accomplish
▶ be realistic and attainable
▶ have a definite point of completion (long-term goals should be broken up into short-term goals with definite target completion dates)

▶ be flexible; sometimes great opportunities come along that take you in new directions, but still lead toward your long-term goals

If you have never thought through your career path before, you may be surprised by the direction it seems to point you in. The process of thinking and writing down your goals can help to clarify what has been unacknowledged all along; you have had many thoughts and feelings about future employment, but until you began to piece them together, they may not have seemed coherent. Once you are armed with this knowledge, you can begin the job search process with greater confidence: you know what you want, and where you want to be. That alone can set you apart from the competition when it comes time to apply for a position.

TAKING A DEADLINE-ORIENTED APPROACH TO YOUR JOB SEARCH EFFORTS

As we have already discussed, landing a job can be a difficult task. You have to find job opportunities, create a resume, write cover letters, schedule interviews, perform research on companies, participate in interviews, make follow up calls, and keep track of all the potential employers you meet or correspond with. One way to help take the stress out of this whole procedure is to adopt an organized, deadline-oriented approach for finding a job as a hotel or restaurant manager.

Begin by purchasing (if you don't already own one) a personal planner such as a Day-Timer®, or a personal digital assistant (PDA) such as a Palm Pilot™ (www.palm.com). Before actually starting your job search, make a list of everything you will have to accomplish in order to land a job. Break up the big tasks into lots of smaller ones, which are easier to accomplish. Items you will probably put on your list include:

▶ writing or updating your resume
▶ getting your resume printed
▶ purchasing outfits to wear to interviews
▶ following up with interviewers post-interview

Once your list is complete, write down how long you think each task will take to accomplish.

Next, prioritize your list. Determine which tasks need immediate attention, and which items can wait until later in the job search process. When you know what needs to be done and approximately how long it will take to accomplish each task, create a schedule for yourself and set deadlines.

Using your personal planner, calendar, or PDA, start at today's date and enter in each job search-related task, one at a time. Under your list of tasks to complete, add items like "check the help wanted ads" and "update resume." Leave yourself enough time to accomplish each one, and in your planner, mark down the date by which each should be completed.

Keep meticulous notes in your planner or on your PDA. Write down everything you do, with whom you make contact, the phone numbers and addresses of your contacts, topics of discussion on the phone or during interviews, the follow up actions that need to be taken, and even what you wore to each interview. Throughout your job search process, keep your planner or PDA with you at all times. Refer to it and update it often to insure that you remain on track.

Bring your planner or PDA to job interviews, and don't be afraid to jot down notes during the interview. If the interviewer wants to meet with you again, take out your planner or PDA, and make the appointment on the spot. Not only will you be organized, but you will also demonstrate this important quality to a potential employer.

RESEARCHING THE FIELD

Finding the right job always begins with research. You need to know exactly what hotel or restaurant management jobs you are qualified to fill, what jobs are available, where the jobs can be found, and how to land one of those jobs. As stated in previous chapters, hotel or restaurant managers are employed in many settings, from small, privately-owned establishments, to institutions such as schools and prisons, to large corporations owning thousands of sites. Four of the major employers of hotel or restaurant managers (corporations and small businesses, colleges and universities, healthcare facilities, and resorts, spas, and cruise lines) are examined next, along with

resources for finding the information you will want to have about a potential employer, including:

▶ amount of pay and quality of benefits compared to market norms
▶ level of formality and flexibility in the workplace culture
▶ whether there are training programs available to help employees
upgrade their skills
▶ promotion and raise policies and track records
▶ level of "family friendliness" (flex time for children's doctor's visits,
whether child care facilities are available on the premises, and so forth)
▶ substantiated complaints against the company
▶ awards won by the company

While doing your research, keep the following questions in mind:

1. What is the organization's financial condition? You will want to look
for an employer with a solid track record and sound business practices
that add up to a stable financial future.
2. Is the organization's business or activity consistent with your own
interests and ethics? Obviously, it is easier and more pleasant to go to
work if you are enthusiastic about what the organization does.
3. How will the size of the organization affect you? Large companies
generally offer a greater variety of training programs and career
paths, more levels to advance to, and better employee benefits than
small firms. Large employers may also have better facilities and
equipment. However, jobs in large companies are often very specialized, whereas jobs in small companies may offer more variety and
responsibility, a closer working relationship with management, and a
chance to see your contribution to the success of the organization.
4. Should you work for a new small business or for one that is well established? New small businesses have a high failure rate, but for many
people, the excitement of getting in on the ground floor and the
potential for sharing in its success makes up for the risk of job loss.
5. Where is the job located? If it is in another city, is the cost of living
higher than you are used to? What about the availability of housing
and transportation, and the quality of educational and recreational

facilities in the new location? Will there be excessive commuting time?

You can also get valuable information from industry associations. For instance, the National Restaurant Association sponsors state associations that can provide you with information about the market in your area, and the employment prospects within it. Log onto their website at www. restaurant.org/states for contact information. A list of other associations may be found in Appendix A at the end of this book.

Corporations and Small Businesses

The easiest way to get background information on a company is to contact it directly. Larger corporations, and even some small businesses, maintain websites that contain much of the information you will be looking for. You might also try telephoning a company's public relations office and asking for information. Ask for a copy of the company's annual report to the stockholders, which describes its corporate philosophy, history, products or services, goals, and financial status. Press releases, company newsletters or magazines, and recruitment brochures also can be helpful.

Background information on the organization may be available at your public or school library. If you cannot get an annual report, check the library for reference directories that provide basic facts about the company, such as earnings, products and services, and number of employees. Some directories that are widely available in libraries include the following:

Dun & Bradstreet's Million Dollar Directory
Standard and Poor's Register of Corporations
Directors and Executives
Moody's Industrial Manual
Thomas' Register of American Manufacturers
Ward's Business Directory

The Internet is also an excellent resource for researching potential employers. To find lists of employers in the hospitality industry, try websites geared toward business news and information, such as www.business.com. Check out some of these other sites, which may be useful in finding the information you are looking for:

www.analysiszone.com
www.businessjeeves.com/MoneyComInd.html
www.corporateinformation.com
www.companydescriptions.com
www.planetbiz.com

Don't forget your school's placement office, which should also have information about nearby businesses that employ hotel or restaurant managers. They may even have valuable contacts with companies that routinely hire their graduates.

Colleges and Universities

There are thousands of colleges and universities in the United States, each employing food service managers, catering managers, and/or dining services directors. How can you learn more about these potential employers? Begin by going back to page 41 of this book, in which there is a list of online college guides. You can use many of these sites to conduct searches for schools based on a number of criteria, including geographic location and size of the institution. Your library will also have the latest college guidebooks, and catalogues from schools in your area. Once you have made a list of schools at which you are interested in working, contact them directly for more information.

You may also want to check out the National Association of College and University Food Services (NACUFS). This organization is comprised of food service professionals from over 650 colleges and universities. It offers educational opportunities, networking, and job bulletins.

Healthcare Facilities

Possibilities for jobs in the healthcare industry include working for hospitals, nursing homes, and short- and long-term care facilities, all of which employ housekeeping and food service managers (titles may vary). There are also many contract food service companies that provide management service to healthcare facilities. To find locations in your area, you can check with your local library or the Yellow Pages. www.hospitallink.com is also a good resource; it contains links to hundreds of hospitals' websites, and is organized by state.

When researching the business of healthcare facilities, a good site to check out is the previously mentioned www.business.com. Their "Healthcare Facilities and Health Systems" page contains links to hundreds of sites, including those of industry associations, hospitals, and long-term care facilities. You can get financial, background, and contact information for thousands of these facilities, as well as for the contract food service operators that provide services to many of them.

If you are interested in a job with a contract food service operator that does business primarily with the healthcare industry, consider contacting one or more of the following companies. By doing so, you can get a better idea of this sector of the market, even if you are not interested in working for one of them specifically.

HDS Service
39395 West 12 Mile Road, Suite 101
Farmington Hills, MI 48331-2967
800-899-8826
www.hdsservices.com

Morrison Management Specialists
1955 Lake Park Drive, Suite 400
Smyrna, GA 30080-8855
770-437-3300
www.iammorrison.com

Nutrition Management Services
725 Kimberton Road
Kimberton, PA 19442
610-935-2050
www.nmsc.com

For more information, you may want to contact one of the industry associations, which provide opportunities for education and networking—a great way to learn more about healthcare positions (see the section on Networking later in this chapter). Two worth contacting are:

The American Society For Healthcare Food Service Administrators
One North Franklin
Chicago, IL 60606
312-422-3870; fax: 312-422-4581
www.ashfsa.org

The National Society for Healthcare Food Service Management
204 E Street NE
Washington, D.C. 20002
202-546-7236; fax: 202-547-6348
www.hfm.org

The Resort Industry

The resort industry is made up of a number of sectors, including ski/mountain resorts, beach resorts, theme parks, spas, clubs, casinos, and cruise lines; there are resorts that cater to golfers, scuba divers, tennis players, fishermen, and horseback riders. Most of these locations employ hotel and restaurant managers. When researching the industry for hospitality employment, keep in mind that resorts are usually corporately owned. Once you have narrowed down the area(s) in which you have an interest, you can find out about potential employers as you would if seeking a position with any corporately owned hotel or restaurant. Check back to page 97 for advice on gathering information about such employers. In addition, many of the online resources listed later in this chapter, especially those that deal specifically with the hospitality industry, contain job information and company profiles that may be of interest.

Other ways to research the resort industry include the use of travel and leisure publications. Libraries usually have many of these resources, and may be especially helpful if you are interested in a local resort. There are also a number of travel websites that contain information on resorts, including:

www.casinoemployment.com
www.casinogambling.about.com
www.resortsandlodges.com
www.resortsource.com
www.ski-guide.com
www.skiresortguide.com
www.spafinder.com
www.spaindex.com
www.vacation-hotline.com/resorts.htm

If you are interested in cruise line employment, your research will need to be somewhat different. Cruise ships are like floating hotels, and indeed, they employ hotel and restaurant managers much as a business would do on land. However, learning about job opportunities can be tricky. If you begin searching on the Internet, you will notice a number of products and services which purport to help you land cruise line jobs; they charge you a fee for printed material, an "application," a list of available cruise jobs, or a "placement" service that guarantees you will get a job. However, according to those who have work experience on ships, paying to find a job with a cruise line is unnecessary. In fact, some of the services are in business simply to take your money.

It is better to deal directly with the cruise lines, which maintain websites that give out plenty of information about their business, including employment opportunities. You will notice that some companies use agencies to fill certain types of positions, while others have labor agreements with unions in countries other than the United States (thus large numbers of job openings are only available to members of these unions). But, the majority of hotel and food service positions, which involve direct contact with the mostly English-speaking guests, are filled by Americans, Canadians, and British citizens.

Use the list below to research some of the largest cruise lines. The business websites listed in the previous section on Corporations and Small Businesses are also worth checking out. You may want to read travel and resort publications, such as *Travel and Leisure* magazine, which rates cruise lines, and gives detailed (and less biased) descriptions of their services and reputations. You can also search the Internet with the terms "cruise and employment" to find more information. (Remember to beware of products or services that charge you money!)

Carnival Cruises: www.carnival.com
Celebrity Cruises: www.celebrity-cruises.com
Cunard: www.cunardline.com
Disney: www.disney.go.com/DisneyCruise
Holland America: www.hollandamerica.com
Princess Cruises: www.princesscruises.com
Radisson Seven Seas Cruises: www.rssc.com
Royal Caribbean cruise line: www.rccl.com

FINDING THE JOBS AVAILABLE

There are a number of great ways to locate employment as a hotel or restaurant manager. Some have been around for years, such as classified ads and job placement firms. Others are more recent additions to the job search arena, and offer great possibilities. They include such Internet resources as industry-specific sites, some of which list employment opportunities, and general career-related websites.

School Career Placement Centers

Almost every school has a career placement center, whose director has the job of helping you to find employment when you graduate. A good placement office will have directories of businesses in the local area, information about job fairs, and copies of any industry publications that list hotel or restaurant manager job openings. A top placement director also maintains contacts with the business community, making his or her office one of the first places to hear about a job opening. The placement office is a great place to find valuable general information about the market in your area.

Classified Ads

Conventional job-hunting wisdom says you shouldn't depend too much on classified ads for finding a job. However, this resource shouldn't be overlooked, especially if you are still in school. By reading the classifieds, you can learn valuable information about the market for hotel or restaurant managers in your area. For instance, you will see at least a partial list of the places that hire hotel or restaurant managers.

You can also get an idea of typical salaries and benefits in your area. Since one of the hardest questions to answer on an application or in an interview is: "What is your desired salary?" it can be worthwhile to watch the ads and know the going rate ahead of time. You can also get information about temporary and part-time jobs, which are very common ways for hotel or restaurant managers to begin their careers.

In addition to the educational aspect of classified ads, reading and responding to them may actually lead to a position. Many companies advertise hotel or restaurant manager positions in the classifieds primarily because it is an inexpensive way to reach a large number of potential applicants. However, that means that, depending on your area, dozens of applicants will send a resume to the employer, and you will be competing with all of them. Don't wait to respond. If the ad appears in the Sunday newspaper, respond to it on Monday morning. Used properly, the classifieds not only improve your knowledge of the job market, but can lead to your first position as a hotel or restaurant manager.

Job Directories

While the Internet has probably surpassed the library in terms of usefulness in your job search, your local library and chamber of commerce are also good places to look. Both maintain directories of employers in your area. Two excellent sources organized specifically for job hunters are *The World Almanac National Job Finder's Guide* (St. Martin's Press) and the *Job Bank* series (Adams, Inc.). There are brief job descriptions and online resources in the *Job Finder's Guide*; the *Job Bank* books are published by geographic region and contain a section profiling specific companies, with contact information for major employers in your region sorted by industry; for example, *Atlanta Job Bank*.

Once you have identified companies in your area of interest, use the resources at your local library to learn more about them. Your librarian can help you find public information about local businesses, including the names of all the company's officers, the number of employees, a brief description of the company, and contact information.

Employment or Personnel Agencies

Employment agencies place managers in full-time positions (as opposed to temporary agencies, which offer short- or long-term temporary positions). Be sure to find out who is responsible for paying their fee before you sign up with an agency; some charge you, while others collect fees from your new employer. While placement agencies may work extensively with you before finding you a job (fine-tuning your resume, holding practice interviews, testing your skills), your relationship with the agency ends once you are placed with an employer. To find job placement firms in your area, search the Internet with the terms "employment agency" and "hotel or restaurant manager."

Job Fairs

Attending job or career fairs is another way to find employment. Job fairs bring together a number of employers under one roof, usually at a hotel, convention center, or civic center. These employers send representatives to the fair to inform prospective employees about their company, to accept resumes, and, occasionally, to conduct interviews for open positions. Many fairs are held specifically for hotel or restaurant management employers and prospective employees. They usually hold seminars for attendees covering such topics as resume writing, job hunting strategies, and interviewing skills.

Your school may also conduct job fairs. Some hotel and food service management departments invite representatives from dozens of companies and local businesses each year before graduation. The emphasis at these fairs is usually on interviews; you can sign up for interviews with any or all of the attending companies, and gain valuable experience in the process. If your school does not hold job fairs, contact the information office of the convention center or civic center nearest you and ask if there is one on their upcoming events calendar. The local newspaper or state unemployment office may also have relevant information. And check the Internet with the search terms "job fair" and "hotel or restaurant manager."

While it is true that you will most likely be competing with many other job seekers at a job fair, your ability to impress an employer is far greater during an in-person meeting than it is if you simply respond to a help wanted ad by submitting your resume. By attending a job fair, your appearance, level of preparation, what you say and how you say it, and your body language can be used to help make an employer interested in hiring you. When attending a job fair (other than one held at the school you are attending), your goal is to get invited to come in later for a formal in-person interview. Keep in mind that time is limited with an employer at a job fair, typically between five and ten minutes, and although it is very rare that an employer will hire someone on the spot, this can happen.

Preparation on your part is vital. Determine beforehand which employers will be there and whether or not you have the qualifications to fill the job openings available. Begin your research by visiting the website created to promote the job fair you are interested in attending. The website typically lists detailed information about the firms attending and what types of jobs participating employers are looking to fill. Once you pinpoint the firms you are interested in, research them as if you are preparing for an actual in-person job interview.

Determine exactly how your qualifications and skills meet the needs of employers in which you are interested. Also, develop a list of questions to ask the employer during your in-person meeting at the job fair. Showing a sincere interest in working for an employer and asking questions that demonstrate your interest will help set you apart from the competition in a positive way.

Bring plenty of copies of your resume to the job fair, and begin by visiting the companies you are most interested in working for. It is best to make contact with these firms as early in the day as possible, when their representatives are fresh and most responsive. They may meet with dozens of potential employees each day, repeating the same information each time. You should be prepared to answer questions about why you want to work for their company and how your skills and qualifications make you qualified to fill one of the positions the employer has available. As you meet with people, collect business cards and follow up your meetings later that day with a short letter, e-mail, or fax thanking the person you met with for their time. Use this correspondence to reaffirm your interest in working for an employer.

Online Resources

As mentioned before in this chapter, one of the fastest growing and most comprehensive resources for job searching is the Internet. There are two types of sites that you should find to be of great use as you look for employment. The first, career-related websites, offer help with every step of the process, from resume writing to researching a firm before accepting a job offer. You may also network with other people in your field, and obtain valuable career-related advice on some of these sites. The second type of site is hotel and restaurant manager-related, and contains lists of job openings geared specifically to your profession.

Career-Related Websites

Some of the online resources available to the job hunter are listed next. But don't limit yourself to this selection; using any Internet search engine or portal (such as www.dogpile.com, www.hotbot.com, or www.yahoo.com), you can enter a keyword such as: "resume," "job," "career," "job listings," or "help wanted" to find thousands of others.

6-Figure Jobs—www.6figurejobs.com
About.com—www.jobsearch.about.com/jobs/jobsearch/msubrespost.htm
America's Employers—www.americasemployers.com
America's Job Bank—www.ajb.dni.us
Boston Herald's Job Find—www.jobfind.com
Career Builder*—www.careerbuilder.com
Career.com—www.career.com
CareerNet—www.careers.org
CareerWeb—www.cweb.com
College Central Network—www.employercentral.com
Gary Will's Worksearch—www.garywill.com/worksearch
JobBank USA—www.jobbankusa.com
JobLynx—www.joblynx.com
JobSource—www.jobsource.com
Monster Board—www.monster.com
Occupational Outlook Handbook—www.stats.bls.gov/oco/oco1000.htm
Salary.com—www.salary.com
Vault.com—www.vaultreports.com/jobBoard/SearchJobs.cfm
Wall Street Journal Careers—www.careers.wsj.com
Yahoo Careers—www.careers.yahoo.com

*CareerBuilder lists ads from major newspapers, including the *Boston Globe, Chicago Tribune, Los Angeles Times, New York Times, San Jose Mercury News, Washington Post, Philadelphia Inquirer,* and *Southern Florida Sun-Sentinel.*

Hotel and Restaurant Manager Employment Sites

Most of these sites list only jobs in your profession; however a few of them are more comprehensive. Conduct a search on the Internet with terms such as "hotel [or restaurant] manager" and "employment" to find more sites.

Ehotelier—www.ehotelier.org
Federal Job Announcements—www.fedworld.gov/jobs/jobsearch.html
Food Service.com—www.foodservice.com
Hotel Manager Jobs—www.hotelmanagerjobs.com
Hospitality Careers—www.hcareers.com
Hospitality Executive—www.hospitalityexecutive.com
Hospitality Online—www.hospitalityonline.com/jobs
National Hospitality Associates—www.nationalhospitality.com
Restaurant Beast—www.restaurantbeast.com
Restaurant Jobs—www.restaurantjobs.com
Restaurant Managers.com—www.restaurantmanagers.com
Restaurant Recruit—www.restaurantrecruit.com
Restaurantville—www.restaurantville.com
SOS hotels—www.soshotels.com

Government Job Searches

Finding a job with the government is a more involved process than finding one at a small business or corporation. While some federal agencies have the authority to test and hire applicants directly, most work through the Office of Personnel Management (OPM), which accepts applications, administers the appropriate written tests, and then submits an eligibility list of qualified candidates to the agency for consideration. For example, if you want a job with The Department of Agriculture, you will have to wait until you see a specific vacancy announcement posted through the OPM, then go through the office to start the application process.

There are several ways to get information from the OPM, with the easiest being through their website at www.opm.gov. On this site, you can read answers to frequently asked questions, read about changes that are affecting government employees, read and download or print some of the forms you may need, and get some background information about the OPM. You can also contact them at 202-606-1800.

The OPM also operates www.usajobs.opm.gov, which lists employment opportunities, including the full text of the job announcement. The announcement will give you the classification of the job, known as a "grade."

It will indicate the experience necessary, salary level, and other features. Once you have read the application process for a specific job, you can access an online application that may be used to create a resume. After creating it, you can submit the resume electronically, or save it to their system to retrieve and edit for future use.

You may also find a food service position with the government at many individual agencies, which do their own hiring and maintain websites that list job openings. *Federal Jobs Digest* maintains a website that claims to be the country's premier source of federal job information. They not only post job openings, but also allow you to register your resume, conduct a job-matching search, and read job descriptions, including the extensive benefits that come with federal employment. Check them out at www.jobsfed.com.

Industry-specific periodicals, such as those listed in the next section, often list federal government job openings, as do national newspapers. You may also get information from a Federal Job Information Center. There is at least one of these centers in each state, which posts federal job openings for the area in which it is located. While many offer only a recording over the telephone or several job announcements posted on the wall, they can be a worthwhile contact.

Industry Newsletters & Magazines

If you are already a member of one or more of the hospitality industry associations, you are familiar with the publications they produce; if not, consult the list in Appendix B. There are hundreds of newsletters and magazines that deal with the industry as a whole, or specific segments of it. Many of them contain classified sections in which job opportunities are listed. This is especially true of those associations that publish material on their websites.

In addition to discovering specific employment openings in industry publications, your reading will help you to track changes and identify trends in the industry. Newsletters and magazines often announce breaking news and explain its significance. Being up on industry news will help convince potential employers that you will be a valuable asset to their business. The following are some helpful periodicals:

National Publications—Broad Industry Coverage
Nation's Restaurant News—weekly, 800-944-4676
Restaurant Business—bimonthly, 212-592-6264
Restaurant Economic Trends—monthly, 202-331-5900
Restaurant Hospitality—monthly, 216-696-7000
Restaurants & Institutions—monthly, 800-446-6551
Restaurants USA—monthly, 202-331-5900

NETWORKING

It is estimated that up to 90% of all jobs are filled by word of mouth. That means that someone you know, perhaps even an acquaintance, may be instrumental in helping get you employed. But that doesn't mean you should sit around waiting for someone to call with a job offer. Instead, be in active contact with those you know, in effect, creating a network, and work your network as an integral part of your job search process.

Described in this way, the process probably sounds a lot less complicated and intimidating than the "networking" you may have heard of. Networking is simply the art of making contact with others to obtain information or get help meeting a specific goal. Successful people know that it is useful throughout a career, both when just starting out, and when looking to move ahead. But there are still some who picture it as insincere small talk or hand-shaking. Don't let that reputation get in the way—when done properly, net-working is completely sincere, and can provide many benefits, such as:

▶ mentoring
▶ making contacts within a hiring company
▶ furthering training
▶ getting information about trends in the industry
▶ increasing business

Todd Warren, director of sales and marketing for a large hotel group, notes that once you are employed, you will need to network with your peers at other lodging establishments. He also offers the following:

Hotels in the same city rely on each other. Even though we are competitors, we need to work together. For instance, if I am sold out, I will send guests to your hotel, and I expect you to do the same for me. It is not uncommon for hotels to call each other and check on availability. If you don't have positive relationships with your competitors, you will miss out on information, and on the business they can send you. Plus, as you get along in your career, you may find yourself working with one or more of them. It pays to network, and be a team player, with your peers in the hospitality industry.

The key to successful networking, no matter where you are in your career, is to break down the process into seven, easy-to-follow steps. An exploration of these steps follows, showing each one's direct application to a hotel or restaurant management job search.

Step One: Identify Small Goals

Your ultimate goal, not only for networking, but for the entire job search process, is to find a great job. However, you shouldn't approach day-to-day networking as a means to that larger goal. Instead, as your first step, identify smaller goals that can be met quickly. For instance, suppose you have narrowed down your search to three hotels in your area. Now, you want to get "inside" information about them in order to decide which to apply for a job with. Or, you may simply be seeking advice from those already working in the field. Once your goals are identified, you can best determine how to meet them.

Step Two: Be Informed

If your goal is to seek advice about employers in your area, get as much information as you can first. Research the companies that hire hotel or restaurant managers as described earlier in this chapter. Understand the field in general, too. You want to sound like you have done your homework when you begin to make contacts.

This is also the step in which you should begin to make a list of potential contacts that may help you meet your goal(s). If you are in school, the person running the Job Placement Office should be at the head of your list. Then, look to your research: you have probably read the names of others you can add to your list (heads of human resource departments, and others who do the hiring for their businesses). Others who may be of help to you are:

▶ friends and relatives
▶ current or former fellow students
▶ current or former teachers
▶ other members of professional associations
▶ other professionals, such as your insurance agent
▶ people who work for a company you would like to work for

Newsletters from your industry associations may list hotel or restaurant managers working in your area. The Internet is also a good place to find contacts. Industry association websites may provide you with leads, and there are an increasing number of sites that provide message boards on which job seekers can network. Check out some of the business sites listed throughout this chapter, and find other sites by searching the Internet with terms such as "networking" and "job search."

Step Three: Make a Connection

Using the list of potential contacts you developed in step two, build your network. Connect with each person, and take the time to let him or her know about your job search. Tell them briefly about your education, and what makes you a superior candidate. Give them a good idea about the types of positions you are most interested in. In other words, be sure that everyone you know who may be able to help you land a job knows that you are looking for one!

During these contacts, work on developing a list of hotel or restaurant managers who work at the places where you are interested in finding employment. Call them, or visit them at work. Although busy, most will take a few minutes to speak with a prospective newcomer. They were new to the business once themselves, so if you are careful not to take up too much of their time, they will probably be willing to give you some information. Begin by introducing yourself, showing that you are informed (step two) and interested in what they have to say. Then, ask if they are willing to help you.

Step Four: Ask for What You Want

If your contact indicates that he or she is willing to help you, be honest and direct about what you want. If your goal is to find out inside information about the restaurant in which a contact works, tell her that you are thinking of applying to work there. Then, ask questions such as:

▶ "How do you like the restaurant?"
▶ "What are the benefits of working here?"
▶ "What is the atmosphere like?"
▶ "Where else have you worked, and how does this restaurant compare?"

Step Five: Expand Your Network

One of the most valuable pieces of information you can get from a contact is another contact. After you have received the information you need to meet your step one goal(s), simply ask if he or she would mind sharing with you the name of another person who might also be able to help you.

Also consider requesting informational interviews at hotels or restaurants that interest you. An informational interview is one in which you meet with someone to find out about the company, and may be an excellent opportunity to:

▶ learn more about how the hotel or restaurant works
▶ gain interview experience
▶ make a contact that might help you get a job in the future

You can also expand your circle of contacts by joining professional organizations while you are still a student (many even offer discounted student memberships). Be sure to join both national organizations and their local chapters. Though the national organizations can give you valuable information, it is on the local level that you will be more effective at networking. Go to local meetings and ask questions—people almost always like to talk about their jobs—and volunteer for committees. The members of your local hotel or restaurant manager group will most likely know about job openings before anyone else does.

Step Six: Organize Yourself

You have probably already written down your goals, and made lists of contacts. Once you have spoken with some of them, organization becomes even more important. You will need to keep track of your contacts, as well as the information you receive from them. When you need to connect with this person again in the future, you will be able to easily access your information. There are software packages that can help you to keep track of your networking contacts, or, you can simply use a notebook and organize yourself. For each contact, note:

- ▶ name
- ▶ address
- ▶ e-mail address
- ▶ phone number (work, pager, cellular phone, residence)
- ▶ fax number
- ▶ company name
- ▶ job title
- ▶ first meeting—where, when, the topics you discussed
- ▶ last contact—when, why, and how

Step Seven: Maintain Your Contacts

It is important to maintain your contacts once you have established them. Try to reach people again within a couple of weeks of meeting them. You can send a note of thanks, ask a question, or send a piece of information related to your conversation with them. This contact cements your meeting in their minds, so they will remember you more readily when you call them again in the future. If you haven't communicated with your contacts for a few months, you might send them a note or e-mail about an article you read, relevant new technology, or other information, to keep your name fresh in their minds.

As you begin your job hunt, keep in mind that you are not just looking for a job; you are looking for a good job, one you will enjoy and feel challenged by. Remember: you are not begging for employment; you are trying to find an employer who will be a match for your skills and talents. Once you have found an available position or positions that interest you, you will need to contact potential employers and express your interest. Chapter 5 explains how best to make that contact, from the initial phone call or letter, to the interview and job evaluation.

THE INSIDE TRACK

Who: Lyle Feingold
What: Kitchen Manager
Where: Gray Hill Academy
               Dallas, Texas

INSIDER'S STORY

I'm one of eleven kids, so my mom did a lot of cooking! I always liked helping her in the kitchen, from just stirring or slicing vegetables, to making whole meals by myself when I was older. There's something really satisfying about taking a pile of ingredients and transforming them into something that's both beautiful to look at and delicious.

I trained as a chef—I have an associate's degree in Culinary Arts—and worked as a chef for eight years before I took my current job. I am the kitchen manager at a small private school. The students are divided pretty evenly between boarders and day students, so we provide lunch for all of them, as well as breakfast, dinner, and snacks for the residential students. My experience was very helpful in getting this position; I didn't have any formal management experience, but many of my other jobs had incorporated different management-level responsibilities, so I was already familiar with many facets of the job. The director of dining services is also a graduate of my training program, and I'm sure it was an asset to me that she knew the program and had an idea of the kind of things I would have learned there.

Since we are an educational institution, I pay close attention to the nutritional value of the food we prepare, as well as accommodating the special needs of students who are diabetic, allergic to certain foods, vegan, or vegetarian. Having come from a culinary background, though, I'm also very interested in serving food that's fresh and attractive, and most importantly, tastes good—we want the kids to like it! Working for a private school lets me experiment a little and probably end up with more varied, creative meals than I would if I worked in a public school or larger institution. Since the students are paying quite a bit to be here, there is a real "please the customer" attitude, which is nice for me. One of my favorite parts of my job is the feedback and interaction with students.

I still do a lot of cooking, but being kitchen manager also allows me to have more control over the way the kitchen is run than I did when I was a full-time chef. I do all of the menu planning, supervise two full-time cooks and several part-time kitchen staff, and try to streamline the operations of the kitchen (food prep, scheduling shifts) so that everything operates as efficiently as possible. I also order food and kitchen supplies, and ensure that we are in compliance with sanitation and food safety regulations.

During the summers, while the school is closed, I do catering and cook for special events. It's a nice break from the routines of the school year, and again, it's a great way to branch out and be a little more creative than I might be otherwise. I don't know whether I will want to move up to a higher position, but if I do decide to, I know that this experience will be very useful to me. My advice to someone thinking of following this career path is to make sure that you are really suited to it. Attention to detail is essential, and bear in mind that you can't cut corners, either in terms of the quality of the supplies or the energy you invest. You also have to be able to see the broader picture—all while managing a number of other tasks simultaneously.

CHAPTER five

JOB SEARCH SKILLS

ONCE YOU have pinpointed the job opportunities you are interested in pursuing, you will need to contact your potential employer to express your interest. The way you accomplish that contact can be just as important as your skills and training. This chapter will help insure that the impression you leave is the very best possible, making you stand out as a superior candidate. Then, once you receive a job offer or offers, you will need to evaluate them and make a decision. At the end of the chapter, you will find tips on how to go about this final step on your path to employment.

YOUR FIRST contact with a potential employer may be through a phone call, a mailed cover letter and resume, an e-mailed resume, or an interview. Whatever the form, it is imperative that you use it to make an excellent impression. A resume with even one spelling error, an unprofessional sounding phone call, or an interview to which you arrive ten minutes late can all mean disaster to a job search. Once you are offered a job, you will need to handle the offer professionally, too.

It is not hard to master the job search skills you need to succeed, but it does take some time and effort. By carefully reading this chapter, you will learn how to land the job you want by writing great cover letters and resumes, interviewing with confidence and proficiency, and assessing job offers thoroughly and honestly.

WRITING YOUR RESUME

Whether you are responding to an advertisement, following up on a networking opportunity, or making a cold contact, your resume is usually the first means by which a potential employer learns about you. Think of it as an advertisement you write to help sell yourself. A successful advertisement catches your attention by combining several elements: Content, composition, clarity, and concentration. Falling short in any of these areas can cause a reader to pass over the ad; you want to make sure that a prospective employer will pay attention to yours.

As you write, edit, and proofread your resume, make an effort to keep all of the information short, to the point, and totally relevant. Anything you leave out can be discussed later, during a job interview. The purpose of your resume is to get an employer interested enough in you so you make it to the next level, getting invited for an interview.

Creating a powerful resume will take time and effort. Even if you have written dozens before, it is worth the effort to seek out good resume-writing resources to help you draft one for your new career as a hotel or restaurant manager. While much has remained the same over the years, there are current standards and trends for resumes, including e-mailable and computer scannable resumes, that you should know about.

To start, check out your school's placement office, which may have copies of former students' resumes. Books such as *Great Resume* by Jason R. Rich (LearningExpress, 2000) contain excellent general guidelines. And there are plenty of online resources to help you create a winning resume, including the following:

- ▶ ABA Resume Writing—www.abastaff.com/career/resume/resume.htm
- ▶ Accent Resume Writing—www.accent-resume-writing.com/critiques
- ▶ Damn Good Resume—www.damngood.com/jobseekers/tips.html
- ▶ The Elegant Resume—http://resumeadvice.tripod.com
- ▶ e Resume Writing—www.eresumewriting.com
- ▶ JobStar—www.jobstar.org/tools/resume
- ▶ JobWeb—www.jobweb.com/catapult/guenov/restips.html
- ▶ Learn2 Write a Resume—www.learn2.com/07/0768/0768.asp

- ▶ Monster.com Resume Center—resume.monster.com
- ▶ Rebecca Smith's eResumes & Resources—www.eresumes.com
- ▶ Resumania—www.resumania.com
- ▶ Resume Magic—www.liglobal.com/b_c/career/res.shtml
- ▶ Resume Tutor—www1.umn.edu/ohr/ecep/resume
- ▶ Resume Workshop—http://owl.english.purdue.edu/workshops/ hypertext/ResumeW/index.html
- ▶ 10 Minute Resume—www.10minuteresume.com

The four elements of resume writing—content, composition, clarity, and concentration—are discussed next in greater detail.

Content

Use the following questionnaire to gather the information you will need for your resume. In the following sections, you will learn how to organize, format, and word it to make the best possible impression.

Contact Information

The only personal information that belongs on your resume is your name (on every page, if your resume exceeds one page in length), address, phone number, and fax number and e-mail address if you have them. Under no circumstances should you include personal information such as age, gender, religion, health or marital status, or number of children.

Full name:_____

Permanent street address:_____

City, State, Zip:_____

Daytime telephone number:_____

Evening telephone number:_____

Pager/cell phone number (optional):_____

Fax number (optional):_____

E-mail address:_____

Personal website address/online portfolio URL:_____

School address (if applicable): _____

_____

Your phone number at school (if applicable): _____

Job/Career Objective(s)

Write a short description of the job you are seeking. Be sure to include as
much information as possible about how you can use your skills to the
employer's benefit. Later, you will condense this answer into one short sentence. _____

_____

_____

_____

What is the job title you are looking to fill? _____

_____

Educational Background

Be sure to include any internships in this section. For many recent graduates, it is their only work experience. Include the skills you learned which
will be applicable to the position for which you are applying.

List the most recent college or university you have attended: _____

_____

City/State: _____

What year did you start?: _____

Graduation month/year: _____

Degree(s) and/or award(s) earned: _____

Your major: _____

Your minor(s): _____

List some of your most impressive accomplishments, extracurricular activities, club affiliations, etc.: _____

_____

List computer courses you have taken that help qualify you for the job you
are seeking: _____

_____

_____

Grade point average (GPA): _____

Other college/university you have attended: _____

City/State: _____

What year did you start?: _____

Graduation month/year: _____

Degree(s) and/or award(s) earned: _____

Your major: _____

Your minor(s): _____

List some of your most impressive accomplishments, extracurricular activities, club affiliations, etc.: _____

_____

List computer courses you have taken that help qualify you for the job you are seeking: _____

_____

_____

Grade point average (GPA): _____

High school attended: _____

City/State: _____

Graduation date: _____

Grade point average (GPA): _____

List the names and phone numbers of one or two current or past professors/teachers (or guidance counselors) you can contact about obtaining a letter of recommendation or list as a reference: _____

_____

_____

_____

Personal Skills and Abilities

Your personal skill set (the combination of skills you possess) is something that differentiates you from everyone else. Skills that are marketable in the workplace aren't always taught in school, however. Your ability to manage people, stay cool under pressure, remain organized, surf the Internet, use software applications, speak in public, communicate well in writing, communicate in multiple languages, or perform research are all examples of marketable skills. When reading job descriptions or help wanted ads, pay careful attention to the wording used to describe what the employer is looking for. As you customize your resume for a specific employer, you will want to match up what the employer is looking for with your own qualifications as closely as possible. Try to utilize the wording provided by the employer within the classified ad or job description.

What do you believe is your most marketable skill? Why? _____

_____

_____

_____

List three or four specific examples of how you have used this skill in the past while at work. What was accomplished as a result?

1. _____

2. _____

3. _____

4. _____

What are keywords or buzzwords that can be used to describe your skill?

_____

_____

_____

What is another of your marketable skills? _____

_____

Provide at least three examples of how you have used this skill in the workplace:

1. _____

2. _____

3. _____

What unusual or unique skill(s) do you possess that help you stand out from other applicants applying for the same types of positions as you?

_____

_____

_____

How have you already proven this skill is useful in the workplace?

_____

What computer skills do you possess? _____

_____

What computer software packages are you proficient in (such as Microsoft Office, Meeting Matrix, PowerPoint, Menu Maker, etc.)? _____

_____

_____

Thinking carefully, what skills do you believe you currently lack?

_____

_____

What skills do you have, but need to be polished or enhanced in order to make you a more appealing candidate? _____

_____

What options are available to you to either obtain or to brush up on the skills you believe need improvement (for example: evening/weekend classes at a college or university, adult education classes, seminars, books, home study courses, on-the-job-training, etc.)? _____

_____

_____

_____

In what time frame could you realistically obtain this training?

_____

_____

Work/Employment History

Previous work experience is very important. Even if it had nothing to do with your chosen field, every job taught you something that will make you a better hotel or restaurant manager. Experience in other fields such as medicine, accounting, real estate, human resources, and insurance, is considered a hiring plus by potential employers. Don't overlook or discount volunteer work for the same reason. You gained skills and experience, and your volunteering also indicates that you are committed to your community. (Keep this in mind as you go through your training; if you are short on experience, you might think about volunteering.)

Complete the following employment-related questions for all of your previous employers, including part-time or summer jobs held while in school, as well as temporary jobs, internships, and volunteering. You probably won't want to reveal your past earning history to a potential employer, but you may want this information available as reference when you begin negotiating your future salary, benefits, and overall compensation package.

Most recent employer: _____

City, State: _____

Year you began work: _____

Year you stopped working (write "Present" if still employed): _____

Job title: _____

Job description: _____

_____

_____

Reason for leaving: _____

_____

_____

What were your three proudest accomplishments while holding this job?

1. _____

2. _____

3. _____

Contact person at the company who can provide a reference: _____

_____

Contact person's phone number: _____

Annual salary earned: _____

Employer: _____

City, State: _____

Year you began work: _____

Year you stopped working (write "Present" if still employed): _____

Job title: _____

Job description: _____

_____

_____

Reason for leaving: _____

_____

_____

What were your three proudest accomplishments while holding this job?

1. _____

2. _____

3. _____

Contact person at the company who can provide a reference:_____

_____

Contact person's phone number:_____

Annual salary earned:_____

Military Service (if applicable)

Branch of service you served in:_____

Years served:_____

Highest rank achieved:_____

Decorations or awards earned:_____

Special skills or training obtained:_____

Professional Accreditations and Licenses

List any and all of the professional accreditations and/or licenses you have earned thus far in your career. Be sure to highlight items that directly relate to the job(s) you will be applying for. _____

_____

_____

Hobbies and Special Interests

You may have life experience that should be emphasized for potential employers. Did you help a spouse in a business? Were you a candidate for public office? Any number of experiences can add to your attractiveness as a job candidate. If you don't have a great deal of work experience, this part of your resume is very important. Think about the things you have done. Which have taught you lessons that are valuable for a hotel or restaurant manager to know? If you can't find a way to include those experiences on your resume, mention them in your cover letter.

List any hobbies or special interests you have that are not necessarily work-related, but that potentially could separate you from the competition. Can any of the skills utilized in your hobby be adapted for the workplace?

_____

_____

What non-professional clubs or organizations do you belong to or actively participate in? _____

_____

_____

Personal/Professional Ambitions

You may not want to share these on your resume, but answering the following questions will help you to focus your search, and prepare for possible interviewing topics.

What are your long-term goals?
Personal:_____

_____

_____

Professional:_____

_____

_____

Financial:_____

_____

_____

For your personal, professional, and then financial goals, what are five smaller, short-term goals you can begin working toward achieving right now that will help you ultimately achieve each of your long-term goals?

Short-Term Personal Goals:
1._____
2._____
3._____
4._____
5._____

Short-Term Professional Goals:

1. _____
2. _____
3. _____
4. _____
5. _____

Short-Term Financial Goals:

1. _____
2. _____
3. _____
4. _____
5. _____

Will the job(s) you will be applying for help you achieve your long-term goals and objectives? If 'yes,' how? If 'no,' why not? _____

_____

_____

_____

Describe your personal, professional, and financial situation right now:

_____

_____

_____

What would you most like to improve about your life overall? _____

_____

_____

What are a few things you can do, starting immediately, to bring about positive changes in your personal, professional or financial life? _____

_____

_____

_____

Where would you like to be personally, professionally, and financially five and ten years down the road? _____

_____

_____

_____

What needs to be done to achieve these long-term goals or objectives?

_____

_____

_____

_____

What are some of the qualities about your personality that you are most
    proud of? _____

_____

_____

_____

What are some of the qualities about your personality that you believe need
    improvement? _____

_____

_____

_____

What do others most like about you? _____

_____

_____

_____

What do you think others least like about you? _____

_____

_____

_____

If you decided to pursue additional education, what would you study and
    why? How would this help you professionally? _____

_____

_____

_____

If you had more free time, what would you spend it doing? _____

_____

_____

_____

List several accomplishments in your personal and professional life that you are most proud of. Why did you choose these things?

1. _____

2. _____

3. _____

4. _____

5. _____

What were your strongest and favorite subjects in school? Is there a way to incorporate these interests into the job(s) or career path you are pursuing?

_____

_____

_____

_____

What do you believe is your biggest weakness? Why wouldn't an employer hire you? _____

_____

_____

_____

What would be the ideal atmosphere for you to work in? Do you prefer a large corporate atmosphere, working at home, or working in a small office?

_____

_____

_____

List five qualities about a new job that would make it the ideal employment opportunity for you:

1. _____

2. _____

3. _____

4. _____

5. _____

What did you like most about the last place you worked? _____

_____

_____

What did you like least about the last place you worked? _____

_____

_____

What work-related tasks are you particularly good at? _____

_____

_____

What type of coworkers would you prefer to have? _____

_____

_____

When it comes to work-related benefits and perks, what is most important
   to you? _____

_____

_____

When you are recognized for doing a good job at work, how do you like to
   be rewarded? _____

_____

_____

If you were to write a 'help wanted' ad describing your ideal dream job, what
   would the ad say? _____

_____

_____

_____

Composition

How your resume looks can be as important as what it says. Potential
employers may receive a stack of resumes for one job opening, and they
probably spend less than one minute deciding which to review further and
which to throw away. Even though the hospitality industry is less conservative than, say, the law profession, you still want to achieve an overall look that
is neat, clean, polished, and within standard resume guidelines. However, a
little creativity might get you noticed; for example, try a pale gray paper and
an alternate clear font, such as Arial, Helvetica, or Tahoma. Find out as much
as you can about a potential employer before deviating from the norm,
though, and remember that many major hotel and restaurant chains are corporate businesses used to viewing corporate style resumes.

   Use the tips in the following box to help organize the material you gath-
ered in the questionnaire.

Resume Creation Tips

No matter what type of resume you are putting together, use these tips and strategies to insure your finished document has the most impact possible when a potential employer reads it.

- Always use standard letter-size paper in white, ivory, cream, or another neutral color.

- Include your name, address, and phone number on every page.

- Make sure your name is larger than anything else on the page (example: your name in 14-point font, the rest in 12-point).

- Use a font that is easy to read, such as 12-point Times New Roman.

- Do not use more than three fonts in your resume.

- Edit, edit, edit. Read it forward and backward, and then have friends with good proofreading skills read it. Don't rely heavily on grammar and spell checkers, which can miss errors.

- Use bullet points for items in a list—they highlight your main points, making them hard to miss.

- Use keywords specific to the hospitality industry.

- Avoid using excessive graphics such as boxes, distracting lines, and complex designs.

- Be consistent when using boldface, capitalization, underlining, and italics. If one company name is underlined, make sure all are underlined. Check titles, dates, et cetera.

- Don't list your nationality, race, religion, or gender. Keep your resume as neutral as possible. Your resume is a summary of your skills and abilities.

- Don't put anything personal on your resume such as your birth date, marital status, height, or hobbies.

- One page is best, but do not crowd your resume. Shorten the margins if you need more space; if it is necessary to create a two-page resume, make sure you balance the information on each page. Don't put just one section on the second page. Be careful about where the page break occurs.

- Keep your resume updated. Don't write "9/97 to present" if you ended your job two months ago. Do not cross out or handwrite changes on your resume.

- Understand and remember everything written on your resume. Be able to back up all statements with specific examples.

You can organize the information on your resume in a number of ways, depending on your work history, and how the hiring company wants the resume submitted. The three most common formats are:

▶ Chronological format
▶ Skills format (also known as a functional resume)
▶ Combination of chronological and skills formats

The most common resume format is chronological—you summarize your work experience year-by-year, beginning with your current or most recent employment experience and working backward. For each job, list the dates you were employed, the name and location of the company for which you worked, and the position(s) you held. Work experience is followed by education, which is also organized chronologically.

The skills resume (also known as the functional resume) emphasizes what you can do rather than what you have done. It is useful if you have large gaps in your work history or have relevant skills that would not be properly highlighted in a chronological listing of jobs. The skills resume concentrates on your skills and qualifications. Specific jobs you have held are listed, but they are not the primary focus of this type of resume.

You may decide a combination of the chronological and skills resumes would be best to highlight your education, experience, and talents. A combination resume allows for a mixture of your skills with a chronological list of jobs you have held. You get the best of both resumes. This is an excellent choice for students who have limited work experience and who want to highlight specific skills.

Cruise Line Tip

Special note to those applying for positions with cruise lines: Many large ship-owning companies use different processes for finding employees. Some companies ask for references to be submitted with a resume; others may demand a specific format for your resume. Whatever the instructions, it is vital that you follow them exactly, or your resume may never be considered.

Making Your Resume Computer-Friendly

One of the biggest trends in terms of corporate recruiting is for employers to accept resumes online via e-mail, through one of the career-related web-sites, or via their own website. If you are going to be applying for jobs online or submitting your resume via e-mail, you will need to create an electronic resume (in addition to a traditional printed resume).

Many companies scan all resumes from job applicants using a computer software program with optical character recognition (OCR), and then enter them into a database, where they can be searched using keywords. When e-mailing your electronic resume directly to an employer, as a general rule, the document should be saved in an ASCII, rich text, or plain text file. Contact the employer directly to see which method is preferred.

When sending a resume via e-mail, the message should begin as a cover letter (and contain the same information as a cover letter). You can then either attach the resume file to the e-mail message or paste the resume text within the message. Be sure to include your e-mail address and well as your regular mailing address and phone number(s) within all e-mail correspondence. Never assume an employer will receive your message and simply hit "reply" using their e-mail software to contact you.

Guidelines for Creating an Electronic Resume to Be Saved and Submitted in an ASCII Format

- Set the document's left and right margins so that 6.5 inches of text will be displayed per line. This will ensure that the text won't automatically wrap to the next line (unless you want it to).
- Use a basic, 12-point text font, such as Courier or Times Roman.
- Avoid using bullets or other symbols. Instead, use an asterisk ("*") or a dash ("-"). Instead of using the percentage sign ("%") for example, spell out the word *percent*.
- Use the spell check feature of the software used to create your electronic resume and then proofread the document carefully. Just as applicant tracking software is designed to pick out keywords from your resume that showcase you as a qualified applicant, these same software packages used by employers can

also instantly count the number of typos and spelling errors in your document and report that to an employer as well.

- Avoid using multiple columns, tables, or charts within your document.

- Within the text, avoid abbreviations—spell everything out. For example, use the word "Director," not "Dir.," or "Vice President" as opposed to "VP." In terms of degrees, however, it is acceptable to use terms like "MBA," "B.A.," "Ph.D.," etc.

- Use more than one page, if necessary. The computer can handle two or three, and the more skills you list in this extra space, the more "hits" you will get from the computer (a "hit" occurs when one of your skills matches what the computer is looking for).

Properly formatting your electronic resume is critical to having it scanned or read; however, it is what you say within your resume that will ultimately get you hired. According to Rebecca Smith, M.Ed., author of *Electronic Resumes & Online Networking* (Career Press, 2nd Edition) and companion website (www.eresumes.com):

Keywords are the basis of the electronic search and retrieval process. They provide the context from which to search for a resume in a database, whether the database is a proprietary one that serves a specific purpose, or whether it is a Web-based search engine that serves the general public. Keywords are a tool to quickly browse without having to access the complete text. Keywords are used to identify and retrieve resumes for the user.

Employers and recruiters generally search resume databases using keywords: nouns and phrases that highlight technical and professional areas of expertise, industry-related jargon, projects, achievements, special task forces, and other distinctive features about a prospect's work history.

The emphasis is not on trying to second-guess every possible keyword a recruiter may use to find your resume. Your focus is on selecting and organizing your resume's content in order to highlight those keywords for a variety of online situations. The idea is to identify all possible keywords that are appropriate to your skills and accomplishments that support the kinds of jobs you are looking for. But to do that, you must apply traditional resume writing principles to the concept of extracting those keywords from your resume. Once you have written your resume, then you can identify your strategic keywords based on how you imagine people will search for your resume.

Examples of good keywords are:

Hospitality Management
Banquet Sales
Marketing
Guest Relations
Employee Training
Front Office Management
Occupancy Rate
Guest Services
Convention Management
Reservations
Restaurant
Catering
Menu
Beverage
Point-Of-Service (POS) System
Sanitation Certification
Food Service Management
Chef
Foodservice Management Professional (FMP)
Organized and Dependable
Responsible
Willing to travel
Resourcefulness
Team Player
Flexible
Energetic

Industry-related buzzwords, job-related technical jargon, licenses, and degrees are among the other opportunities you will have to come up with keywords to add to your electronic resume. If you are posting your resume on the Internet, look for the categories that the website uses and make sure you use them too. Be sure the words "hotel manager" or "restaurant manager" appear somewhere on your resume, and use accepted professional jargon.

The keywords you incorporate into your resume should support or be relevant to your job objective. Some of the best places within your resume to incorporate keywords can be:

- ▶ Job titles
- ▶ Responsibilities
- ▶ Accomplishments
- ▶ Skills

An excellent resource for helping you select the best keywords to use within your electronic resume is the *Occupational Outlook Handbook* (published annually by the U.S. Department of Labor). This publication is available, free of charge, online (www.stats.bls.gov); however, a printed edition can also be found at most public libraries.

The following is a list of skills almost any company or organization—from a large national motel chain to a local steak house in Dayton, Ohio—will want in a hotel or restaurant manager, so any that you can include on your resume will give you an edge:

- ▶ basic knowledge of computers—ability to use the latest software programs: Databases, reservation programs, menu programs, staff scheduling programs, etc.
- ▶ flexibility and willingness to work long hours
- ▶ being a team player
- ▶ ability to manage other people
- ▶ ability to handle disgruntled guests and employee disputes
- ▶ understanding of organizational relationships, roles, and functions
- ▶ adeptness at working independently, solving problems, and making decisions
- ▶ organizational skills to order supplies and keep track of inventory
- ▶ ability to handle stress
- ▶ willingness to relocate

Clarity

No matter how attractive your resume is, it won't do you any good if a prospective employer finds it difficult to read. The most important rule of resume writing is: Never send out a resume that contains mistakes. Proofread it several times and use your spell-check. For most people, writing a resume is an ongoing process, so remember to check it over every time you make a change. There is absolutely no excuse for sending out a resume with misspelled words or grammatical errors. After you proofread it, ask one or two friends to read it over, too. If you are uncertain about a grammatical construction, for example, change it.

In addition to checking spelling and grammar, you want to make sure that your resume is well written. Resume writing is quite different from other kinds of writing, and it takes some practice. For one thing, most resumes don't use complete sentences. You wouldn't write, "As manager of the housewares department, I managed 14 employees and was in charge of ordering $2.5 million dollars worth of merchandise annually." Instead you would write, "Managed $2.5 million housewares department with 14 employees." Still, all the other rules of grammar apply to writing a resume. Tenses and numbers need to match, and double negatives and other examples of awkward sentence construction are not acceptable.

It is also important to be concise, to help keep your resume at a manageable size, and to make important information stand out. In the two examples in the previous paragraph, the first requires 23 words; the second, just 8. They convey the same information, but the second does it more efficiently. By being concise and demonstrating good word choice, you highlight the fact that you have skills that are valued highly by employers. The abilities to communicate and organize information well are vital to your future job success, and both can easily be reflected in your resume.

You demonstrate your communication abilities not only by making sure everything is spelled correctly and is grammatically accurate, but also by how well you write your resume. Word choice contributes to the clarity and persuasiveness of your resume. Experts have long recommended using verbs (action words) rather than nouns to promote yourself in a resume. Compare "managed $2.5 million housewares department with 14 employees" to "manager of housewares department." The first sounds much more impressive.

However, there is now one caveat to the verb preference rule. As discussed previously, computer resumes, whether scanned or e-mailed, are searched using keywords. These words tend to be nouns rather than verbs. Thus, when writing this type of resume, follow the keyword guidelines spelled out on page 136.

Concentration

Each time you send out a resume, whether in response to an ad, following up a networking lead, or even a cold contact, you should concentrate on tailoring your approach to the employer you are contacting. This means having more than one resume, or reconfiguring your resume before printing it so that it conforms better to the job opening for which you are applying.

For instance, suppose you are interested in work as a catering director, and your first choice is a position in corporate catering. Your preference for *corporate* catering is due, in part, to your work experience in a large corporation. You might be willing to take a position in the restaurant of a large hotel chain, just to get your foot in the door. Restaurant management, in a corporately owned restaurant chain, might also be worth a try. Corporate catering is your dream job; the others are your next choices. To apply for all of these jobs, you will need to alter your resume at least three times.

The resume for the corporate catering position will stress your prior work experience, the food service skills you learned at your internship, and how well you did in your catering class at school. Although it depends on the format you are using, you may very well stress them in that order. For a restaurant management position in a corporately owned restaurant, you would probably stress your internship and education—but make sure your experience working in a large corporation stands out too. For the hotel kitchen job, you would emphasize your basic coursework and internship experience.

Earlier in this chapter, you filled out a questionnaire that helped gather the information you need to write your resume. By keeping it close at hand, it won't be that difficult to construct a resume that targets a particular job by concentrating your information so that a prospective employer will see that you are a likely candidate for this opening. In many cases, a few changes to a basic resume are enough to make it appropriate for a particular job opening.

A good way to tailor your resume for a particular opening is to imagine what the job would be like. Based on the description of the job, what are the major things you would be expected to do day to day? Compare these things with your inventory of experience and education, and decide how to present your information so that the employer will know that you are capable of doing those tasks.

Finally, make sure you get your resume to the appropriate person in the appropriate way. If you got the person's name through a networking contact, your contact may deliver it or suggest that you deliver it in person; most likely, though, you should mail it. If you are making a cold contact—that is, if you are contacting a firm that you found through your research but that not actively looking to fill a position—make sure you find out the name of the head of the human resources department, or whoever else is doing the hiring, and send your resume to that person. If you are responding to an ad, make sure you do what the ad says. If it directs you to fax your resume, do so. Demonstrate your ability to attend to detail.

Avoid Making These Common Resume Errors

- **Stretching the truth.** A growing number of employers are verifying all resume information. If you are caught lying, you won't be offered a job, or you could be fired later if it is discovered that you weren't truthful.

- **Including any references to money.** This includes past salary or how much you are looking to earn within your resume and cover letter.

- **Including the reasons why you stopped working for an employer, switched jobs, or are currently looking for a new job.** Do not include a line in your resume saying, "Unemployed" or "Out of Work" along with the corresponding dates in order to fill a time gap.

- **Having a typo or grammatical error in a resume.** If you refuse to take the time necessary to proofread your resume, why should an employer assume you would take the time needed to do your job properly if you are hired?

■ **Using long paragraphs to describe past work experience.** Consider using a bulleted list instead, which highlights important information. Remember that most employers will spend less than one minute initially reading a resume.

Following are some sample resumes. The first is chronological, which highlights previous experience rather than education. The second is a skills resume; this applicant acquired many of the skills necessary for the position for which he is applying through internships held while in school, but has no employment history in the field. In the third resume sample, note the form, which is designed to be scanned.

Joyce Wilson

1562 State Street

Burlington, Vermont 05401

802-555-6646

OBJECTIVE

Degreed professional in the hospitality field with extensive food, beverage, and catering experience seeks position in management.

PROFESSIONAL BACKGROUND

Banquet/Restaurant/Bar Manager

Radisson Hotels, Radisson Burlington—Burlington, Vermont

June 2000–present

Earned rapid promotion based on performance and commitment to this resort hotel's main goals: revenues, profits and service. Coordinate restaurant and catering sales which produce over $1.2 million annually in food and beverage revenues.

Room Service Manager/Restaurant Supervisor

Holiday Inn—Stowe, Vermont

January 1996–June 1998

Began while in college as a banquet server and bartender. Through dedication to company ideals was quickly promoted. Had responsibility of staffing, SOP controls and service upgrades in the restaurant, room service, and catering areas for this 200-room property.

Assistant Lead Line Cook

Manchester Lion—Waterbury, Vermont

September 1995–January 1996

Promoted from server to working in every aspect of food preparation and presentation.

ACADEMIC ACHIEVEMENTS

Bachelor of Science, Hotel/Restaurant Management Major

Champlain College—Burlington, Vermont

January 2000

Stephen Jones

300 W. Cloister Avenue, Apt. 3

Redstone, PA 16842

814-555-9113

JOB OBJECTIVE

To find a management position in the hotel industry.

EDUCATION

The Pennsylvania State University, University Park, PA

B.S., Hotel, Restaurant, and Institutional Management, May 2001

INTERNSHIPS

Penn State Hospitality Services, University Park, PA

Maintenance Line Intern, September 2000–December 2000

Performed various maintenance jobs within the hotel. Assisted with the upkeep of the interior and exterior of the property.

Penn State Hospitality Services, University Park, PA

Property Operations Executive Intern, February 2001–May 2001

Developed general management skills while assisting the Facility Manager in daily activities, including team briefings, scheduling, and management of maintenance staff.

COMPUTER SKILLS

Experience with Microsoft Office and Web design.

CERTIFICATIONS

TIPS—Health Communications, Inc., 2001

ServSafe—National Restaurant Association Educational Foundation, 2001

Dan Jackson

15 Aspen Way

Sheridan, Illinois

309-555-2222

Objectives

Seeking a position in restaurant management.

Education

Illinois State College (1997–2001)

Bachelor of Science degree in Business Administration, with a minor in Food Service Management.

Employment

Restaurant Manager (Cheddar's Inc., May 2001—Present):

Responsible for every aspect of running the restaurant including:

Human resource management (hiring, training, scheduling, and corrective action)

- Product ordering and receiving
- Quality and inventory control
- Cost analysis and control

Training Coordinator (Chili's, 1995–1997)

Responsible for all employee training (bartenders, servers, hostesses, bussers)

Held regular meetings and evaluated the performance and ability of both the trainees and trainers.

Bartender and Server (Chili's, 1992–1995) Learned legendary customer service and public relations in a high volume restaurant.

Professional

Earned Food Management Professional certification.

WRITING COVER LETTERS

Never send out a resume without a cover letter. The cover letter aims your resume directly at the available job; your resume, in turn, describes in detail why you are the person for the job. If your cover letter is a failure, your resume may not be looked at—at all. As an "introduction" to your resume, the cover letter should give the impression that you are a good candidate for the job. The four elements of the resume—composition, clarity, content, and concentration—apply to cover letters as well. However, because the cover letter has a different function, these elements have some different functions.

Composition

Your cover letter needs to grab the attention of the reader, while remaining within the guidelines discussed previously. As with your resume, avoid loud fonts and stationery; choose styles and paper that matches with your resume. Your cover letter should always be typed (printed) on good paper, using letterhead with your name, address, phone and fax numbers, and e-mail address. Letterhead stationery can be created on your computer rather than ordered through a printing company.

A cover letter should be composed as you would a business letter. It should include the date, the name and address of the person the letter is to be sent to, and a salutation. At the end of the body of the letter, include a closing (such as "Sincerely"), your signature, and your name typed out below. You may use block paragraphs or choose to indent them. It is acceptable to type "enclosure" at the bottom, indicating there is material (your resume) enclosed with the letter.

Your cover letter should not exceed one page unless the employer specifically asks for more information than can reasonably fit. On occasion, an advertisement for a job will ask for a resume and a detailed statement of interest (or words to that effect). Sometimes ads will even ask you to address specific questions or issues in your letter, such as your goals, or what you can contribute to the organization. In such cases, you may need to write a letter that is more than one page.

Clarity

As with your resume, never send out a cover letter with a grammatical or spelling error. Even when you are pressed for time and rushing to get a letter out, make sure to spell-check it and proofread it carefully. Ask someone else to look it over as well. Your letter should be accurate, clear, and concise. It serves as a letter of introduction, an extension of your "advertisement," and it needs to convince a prospective employer that you should be interviewed for the position.

Begin your cover letter with an introduction, followed by an explanation of why you are right for this job, and end with a closing paragraph. As with your resume, it is vital that your cover letter be well written; however, it requires a different writing style. Sentence fragments don't work in a cover letter.

While a resume offers a somewhat formal presentation of your background, a cover letter should let some of your personality come through. View it as your first chance to speak with a prospective employer. The resume tells employers what you know and what you can do; the cover letter should tell them a little bit about who you are. However, even though it is somewhat less formal, avoid using a conversational tone. For example, do not use contractions or slang.

Content and Concentration

While it is important that your resume be tailored to specific job openings, it is even more important to target your cover letter. In fact, its major component should be its concentration on the particular job opening for which you are applying. Because it is so specific, you will need to write a new cover letter every time you send out your resume. It should never read like a form letter, nor should it just repeat the information in your resume. It tells the prospective employer why you are the one for the job.

In the first paragraph, indicate why you are writing the letter at this time. You may write something like:

▶ "I am applying for the position of hotel manager advertised in the April 14, 2002 edition of the Sunday *Post*."
▶ "I am writing in response to your ad in the Sunday, April 14, 2002 edition of the *Los Angeles Times*."
▶ "I am interested in obtaining an entry-level position with your company."
▶ "We met last July at the AH&LA Convention. I will be graduating with my degree in hospitality management in May, and recall that you mentioned you might have an opening for me at that time."

The first paragraph also usually indicates that your resume is enclosed for consideration, although this may also be in the closing paragraph. If you learned about the position from a friend or acquaintance, be sure to mention this mutual contact by name.

In the body of the letter, you want to explain why your training and experience make you the right person for the job. Highlight and summarize the information in your resume, and take advantage of the opportunity to include more about yourself and your skills. For example, life experience that can't be easily incorporated into a resume can smoothly find its way into your cover letter. For example, instead of writing, "Before entering college, I worked at The Motel for two years, and before that at The Hotel for three years," try something like, "I have five years of lodging experience in which I interacted with the public on a daily basis." The body of the letter is your opportunity to explain why the employer should care about your experience and training.

You can also include information about how soon you are available for employment or why (if it is the case) you are applying for a job out of town. You may also mention some of the things that you are looking for in a job—if they are either nonnegotiable or flattering to the employer. Make a direct reference to the specific position and organization. Here are some examples:

▶ "I will graduate on May 16 and will be available for employment immediately. A position with your company appeals to me because your restaurants are known for their wine cellars, and this is an area in which I have experience and am very interested in learning more about."

► "Although my internship was with Marriott International, I have come to realize that while that particular work was intensely interesting, I would prefer employment with a smaller company. Rather than specialize in one small area, a position at a private resort will afford me the opportunity to call on my comprehensive management experience. I believe your hotel is the place for me and I am certain I would be an asset to you."

► "As you look at my resume, you will notice that although I am just now completing my education, I offer a background in guest relations and problem solving. Since your company has recently undergone a major expansion, I believe you would find me a valuable addition to your staff."

Finally, the last paragraph (some people prefer it to be two short paragraphs) should thank the person, make a reference to future contact, and offer to provide further information. Examples of effective closing paragraphs include:

► "Thank you for your consideration. Please contact me at the address or phone number above if you need any further information."

► "I look forward to meeting with you to discuss this job opening."

► "Thank you and I look forward to speaking with you in the near future."

► "I would welcome the opportunity to discuss the match between my skills and your needs in more detail. You can contact me at the address or phone number above, except for the week of the 27th, when I will be out of town. Thank you for your time."

The following is an example of a cover letter utilizing the four components of composition, clarity, content, and concentration.

Dear Mr. Hart:

I am very interested in applying for the restaurant manager position listed in the *Sacramento Register* on May 4, 2001.

As you can see from my enclosed resume, I worked for a large chain restaurant in Reno, Nevada for two years prior to moving to Sacramento. I enjoyed the work very much. I am an organized, detail-oriented person who gets along well with people. I was nominated for Employee of the Year twice in my previous position. I feel that these attributes, along with my work experience, qualify me for the position described in your advertisement.

I would greatly appreciate the opportunity for a personal interview. You can reach me at 555-3944.

Thank you for your consideration.

Sincerely,

Cathy Weston
Enclosure.

INTERVIEWING SUCCESSFULLY

The last step in the job search process, and the one that causes the most anxiety among job seekers, is the interview. A face-to-face meeting with your potential employer gives him or her the chance to decide if you are the right person for the job, and you the chance to decide if the job is right for you. While it is normal to be nervous during an interview, there are many things you can do to calm your fears. The most worthwhile thing you can do is gain a solid understanding of the interview process, and your role in it. By carefully reading the following information, and taking the suggestions made, you will greatly improve your chances for interviewing success.

Be Prepared

Research your potential employer before your interview and be ready to demonstrate your knowledge. Learn about the workings of large chain operations, resorts, institutions, or family-owned businesses. The section in

Chapter 4 entitled "Researching the Field" explained many ways to get the information you are looking for. If you have already done your homework, be sure to refamiliarize yourself just before an interview. If not, now is the time to get the research done.

Preparation should also include practice—find someone to act as an interviewer, and have him or her take you through a mock interview. Ask for an honest evaluation of your performance, and work on those areas your "interviewer" feels you can improve upon.

Act Professionally

Take the interviewing process very seriously. You are entering the professional world, and you want to show that you fit into that environment. Make several extra copies of your resume, letters of recommendation, and your list of references to bring to your interview. You will also want to bring your daily planner, along with your research materials, a pad, and a working pen. All of this paperwork will fit nicely into a briefcase or portfolio. On your pad, write down the company's name, interviewer's name, address, telephone number and directions to the location of the interview.

It is very important to be on time for your interview. Allow extra time for traffic and getting lost if the interview is in an unfamiliar location. Schedule your travel time so that you are in the lobby ten minutes before your interview starts. This will give you time to relax before you begin.

Your appearance is the first thing a potential employer will notice when you arrive for an interview, so make a positive first impression. Be sure that your clothes are free of stains and wrinkles, and that your shoes are shined. If you must make a choice, it is better to be overdressed than underdressed. Personal hygiene is also critical; your hair should be neat, and fingernails clean.

On the morning of your interview, read a local newspaper and watch a morning news program so you are aware of the day's news events and will be able to discuss them with the interviewer. Many interviewers like to start off an interview with small talk. You want to appear knowledgeable about what is happening in the world around you. Also, the beginning of the interview is a great time to ask for the interviewer's business card. Having the card comes in handy when writing thank-you notes and following up. Later in the interview, it's easy to forget to ask for a card.

Speak Confidently

Greet your interviewer with a firm handshake and an enthusiastic smile. Speak with confidence throughout your interview and let your answers convey your assumption that you will be offered the job. For example, phrase your questions this way: "What would my typical day consist of?" "How many managers work here, and what are their areas of responsibility?" Answer questions in complete sentences; however, don't ramble on too long answering any one question. Many hiring managers will ask questions that don't have a right or wrong answer; they ask such questions to evaluate your problem-solving skills.

Keep in mind that a potential employer is not allowed to ask you about your marital status, whether you have children or plan to, your age, your religion, or your race (these kinds of questions may be asked on anonymous affirmative action forms). If you are asked such a question, you can say, "It is illegal for you to ask me that" and then sit silently until the interviewer says something. Or you can say something like, "I don't understand the question; what it is you want to know?" Better yet, figure out why they are asking the question, and address that issue. Then, the answer to "Do you have children?" becomes "If you are asking if I can travel and work overtime, that is not a problem."

Follow these general guidelines when answering questions in an interview:

- ▶ Use complete sentences and proper English.
- ▶ Don't be evasive, especially if you are asked about negative aspects of your employment history.
- ▶ Never imply that a question is "stupid."
- ▶ Don't lie or stretch the truth.
- ▶ Be prepared to answer the same questions multiple times. Make sure your answers are consistent, and never reply, "You already asked me that."

▶ Never apologize for negative information regarding your past.

▶ Avoid talking down to an interviewer, or making them feel less intelligent than you are.

Ask Questions

You will usually be given the opportunity to ask the interviewer questions, so be prepared. Have a list of questions ready in advance. There is much you need to know about the company to determine if it is a good fit for you. It is not a one-way street—while you are being evaluated, you are also evaluating them. If you don't ask any questions, the interviewer may think that you aren't interested in the position.

Almost any type of question is acceptable. You may want to know about the inventory methods and suppliers, whether you will be working under one person or a number of people, or who is responsible for training the housekeeping staff. These are all legitimate questions. You may also have questions about the resources of the company, such as its use of the latest technology and whether employees receive training in its use.

Anticipate the Questions You Will Be Asked

As part of your job interview preparation, think about the types of questions the interviewer will ask. Obviously, since you are applying for a job as a hotel or restaurant manager, you should anticipate detailed questions about the skills you possess and the experience you have using those skills.

Spend time developing well thought out, complete, and intelligent answers. Thinking about them, or even writing out answers on paper will be helpful, but what will benefit you the most is actual practice answering interview questions out loud. Stage a mock interview with someone you trust who will evaluate your responses honestly.

Most of the questions you will be asked will be pretty obvious, but be prepared for an interviewer to ask you a few that are unexpected. By doing this, the interviewer will be able to see how you react and how well you think on your feet.

The following are common interview questions and suggestions on how you can best answer them:

▶ What can you tell me about yourself? (Stress your skills and accomplishments. Avoid talking about your family, hobbies, or topics not relevant to your ability to do the job.)

▶ Why have you chosen to pursue a career as a hotel or restaurant manager? (Give specific reasons and examples.)

▶ In your personal or professional life, what has been your greatest failure? What did you learn from that experience? (Be open and honest. Everyone has had some type of failure. Focus on what you learned from the experience and how it helped you to grow as a person.)

▶ Why did you leave your previous job? (Try to put a positive spin on your answer, especially if you were fired for negative reasons. Company downsizing, a company going out of business, or some other reason that was out of your control is a perfectly acceptable answer. Remember, your answer will probably be verified.)

▶ What would you consider to be your biggest accomplishment at your last job? (Talk about what made you a productive employee and valuable asset to your previous employer. Stress that teamwork was involved in achieving your success, and that you work well with others.)

▶ In college, I see you were an (insert subject) major. Why did you choose (insert subject) as your major? (Explain your interest in the subject matter, where that interest comes from, and how it relates to your current career-related goals.)

▶ What are your long-term goals? (Talk about how you have been following a career path, and where you think this pre-planned career path will take you in the future. Describe how you believe the job you are applying for is a logical step forward.)

▶ Why do you think you are the most qualified person to fill this job? (Focus on the positive things that set you apart from the competition. What is unique about you, your skill set, and past experiences? What work-related experience do you have that relates directly to this job?)

▶ What have you heard about our firm that was of interest to you? (Focus on the firm's reputation. Refer to positive publicity, personal recommendations from employees, or published information that caught your attention. This shows you have done your research.)

▶ What else can you tell me about yourself that isn't listed in your resume? (This is yet another opportunity for you to sell yourself to the employer. Take advantage of the opportunity.)

Avoid Common Interview Mistakes

Once you get invited by a potential employer to come in for an interview, do everything within your power to prepare, and avoid the common mistakes often made by applicants. Remember that for every job you apply for, there are probably dozens of other hotel or restaurant managers who would like to land that same position.

The following are some of the most common mistakes applicants make while preparing for or participating in job interviews, with tips on how to avoid making these mistakes.

▶ **Don't skip steps in your interview preparation.** Just because you have been invited for an interview, you can't afford to "wing it" once you get there. Prior to the interview, spend time doing research about the company, it is products/services and the people you will be meeting with.

▶ **Never arrive late for an interview.** Arriving even five minutes late for a job interview is equivalent to telling an employer you don't want the job. The day before the interview, drive to the interview location and determine exactly how to get there and how long it takes. On the day of the interview, plan on arriving at least ten minutes early and use the restroom before you begin the actual interview.

▶ **Don't neglect your appearance.** First impressions are crucial. Make sure your clothing is wrinkle-free and clean, that your hair is well groomed, and that your make-up (if applicable) looks professional. Always dress up for an interview, even if the dress code at the company is casual. Also, be sure to brush your teeth prior to an interview, especially if you have eaten recently.

▶ **Prior to an interview, avoid drinking any beverages containing caffeine.** Chances are, you will already be nervous about the interview. Drinking coffee or soda won't calm you down.

▶ **Don't go into the interview unprepared.** Prior to the interview, use your research to compile a list of intelligent questions to ask the employer. These questions can be about the company, it is products/services, its methods of doing business, the job responsibilities of the job you are applying for, etc. When it is time for you to answer questions, always use complete sentences.

▶ **Never bring up salary, benefits, or vacation time during the initial interview.** Instead, focus on how you (with all of your skills, experience, and education) can become a valuable asset to the company you are interviewing with. Allow the employer to bring up the compensation package to be offered.

▶ **Refrain from discussing your past earning history or what you are hoping to earn.** An employer typically looks for the best possible employees for the lowest possible price. Let the employer make you an offer first. When asked, tell the interviewer you are looking for a salary/benefits package that is in line with what is standard in the industry for someone with your qualifications and experience. Try to avoid stating an actual dollar figure.

▶ **During the interview, avoid personal topics.** There are questions that an employer can't legally ask during an interview situation (or on an employment application). In addition to these topics, refrain from discussing sex, religion, politics, and any other highly personal topics.

▶ Never insult the interviewer. It is common for an interviewer to ask what you might perceive to be a stupid or irrelevant question. In some cases, the interviewer is simply testing to see how you will respond. Some questions are asked to test your morals or determine your level of honesty. Other types of questions are used simply to see how you will react in a tough situation. Try to avoid getting caught up in trick questions. Never tell or imply to an interviewer that their question is stupid or irrelevant.

▶ Throughout the interview, avoid allowing your body language to get out of control. For example, if you are someone who taps your foot when you are nervous, make sure you are aware of your habit so you can control it during an interview situation.

▶ If your job interview takes place over lunch or dinner, refrain from drinking alcohol of any kind.

Follow Up

It is a common belief that by conducting a job interview, the interviewer is simply doing his or her job, which is to fill the position(s) the employer has available. As a result of this belief, many job seekers show no gratitude to the interviewer. This is a mistake. Sending a personal and well-thought out note immediately after an interview will not only keep your name fresh in the hiring manager's mind, but will also show that you have good follow up skills, and that you are genuinely interested in the job opportunity.

Individual and personalized thank-you notes should be sent out within 24 hours of your interview, to everyone you met with when visiting a potential employer. Send separate notes containing different messages to each person you met with, addressing each using the recipient's full name and title. Make sure you spell names correctly.

Thank-you notes may be typewritten on personal stationery, following a standard business letter format. A more personal alternative is to write your thank-you note on a professional looking note card, which can be purchased at any stationery, greeting card or office supply store. The personal touch will enhance your positive impression and help to separate you from your competition.

Keep your message brief and to the point. Thank the interviewer for taking the time out of his or her busy schedule to meet with you, and for considering you for the job opening available. Make sure you mention the exact position you applied for.

In one or two sentences, highlight the important details discussed during your interview. You want the interviewer to remember you. Don't mention issues under negotiation, such as salary and benefits concerns, or work schedule. Finally, reaffirm your interest in the position and invite further contact with a closing sentence such as "I look forward to hearing from you soon."

Final Thoughts on Interviewing

There are two more important things to keep in mind while going through interviews. Both will help you to keep not only your interview, but the whole job search process, in perspective. The first is that even if you apply and interview for a job, you don't have to take it. The other is that good interviewers try to sell you on coming to work for them.

Understanding that you aren't required to take a job just because it is offered makes the interview seem less like a life-or-death situation and more like an opportunity to get to know at least one person at the hiring company. You will feel a greater sense of confidence and ease when you keep this in mind. The position you are interviewing for isn't the only one available, so if it feels like a bad fit for you, or for them, move on.

Realizing that interviewers should be trying to sell you on coming to work for them is helpful too. A good interviewer has one goal in mind: Finding a good person to fill the job opening. They already think you are a possibility, which is why you were invited to interview. Once you are there, it is the interviewer's job to convince you that you would be very happy working at his or her company. Evaluate the information you are given about the work environment; does it fit with what you see and have heard about the firm? Be attuned to the tactics of the interviewer.

EVALUATING A JOB OFFER

You have been offered the job. Congratulations! Now, you have to decide—or perhaps, choose between a number of offers. How should you go about it? First, take some time. The hiring company or organization will not expect you to accept or reject an offer on the spot; you may be given a weekend or more to make up your mind.

Second, you will need to consider many issues when assessing the offer. This means developing a set of criteria for judging the job offer or offers, whether this is your first job, you are reentering the labor force after a long absence, or you are just planning a change. While determining in advance whether you will like the work may be difficult, the more you find out about it before accepting or rejecting the job offer, the more likely you are to make the right choice. Based on what you learned about the job during your initial research and during your interview, ask yourself the following questions:

► **Does the work match your interests and make good use of your skills?** The duties and responsibilities of the job should have been explained in enough detail during the interview to answer this question.

► **How important is the job to this company?** An explanation of where you fit in the organization and how you are supposed to contribute to its overall objectives should give you an idea of the job's importance.

► **Were you comfortable with the interviewer or with the supervisor you will have (if you met her or him)?**

► **Is this the kind of atmosphere you would enjoy every day?** As you walked through on the way to your interview, or as you were being shown around, did the other employees seem friendly and happy? Did they seem too happy? (If you noticed a party atmosphere, it is possible that not enough is being demanded of them. On the other hand, maybe this is just what you are looking for.) If possible, find out the company's turnover rate, which will indicate how satisfied other employees are with their job and the company.

► **Does the work require travel or possible relocation?** How would this fit into the way you live your life?

► **What hours does the job call for?** In the hospitality industry, you can expect them to be long and irregular, but some employers are better than others at making sure their employees aren't overworked. How are holidays, nights, and weekends staffed? Consider the effect of work hours on your personal life. Also, depending on the job, you may or may not be exempt from laws requiring the employer to compensate you for overtime. Find out how many hours you will be expected to work each week and whether you receive overtime pay or compensatory time off for working more than the specified number of hours in a week.

► **What are the opportunities offered by the job?** A good job usually offers you the opportunity to learn new skills, to increase your earnings, and to rise to a position of greater authority, responsibility, and prestige. A lack of opportunity for betterment can dampen interest in the work and result in frustration and boredom. The person who offers you the job should give you some idea of promotion possibilities within the organization. What is the next step on the career ladder? Is it a step you would want to take? If you have to wait for a job to become vacant before you can be promoted, how long is the wait likely to be? Employers have different policies regarding promotion from within the organization. When opportunities for advancement do arise, will you compete with applicants from outside the company? Can you apply for other jobs in the organization, or is mobility limited?

▶ **What are the salary and benefits?** As noted previously, during the interview, it is best to wait for the interviewer to introduce these subjects. And he or she may not! Many companies will not talk about pay until they have decided to hire you. Once they have made the offer, though, they are bound to mention pay, and in order to know if their offer is reasonable, you need a rough estimate of what the job should pay.

To get an idea of what the salary should be, talk to a friend who was recently hired in a similar job. If you have just finished school, ask your teachers and the staff in the college placement office about starting pay for graduates with your qualifications. Scan the classified ads in newspapers and see what salaries are being offered for similar jobs. Detailed data on wages and benefits are also available from the Bureau of Labor Statistics, Division of Occupational Pay and Employee Benefit Levels, 2 Massachusetts Avenue NE, Room 4160, Washington, DC 20212-0001; 202-606-6225 or online at www.bls.gov. Or, check out Salary.com, and enter a comparable search.

If you are considering the salary and benefits for a job in another geographic area, be sure to make allowances for differences in the cost of living, which may be significantly higher in a large metropolitan area than in a smaller city, town, or rural area. Do take into account that the starting salary is just that, the start. Your salary should be reviewed on a regular basis; many organizations do it every 12 months. How much can you expect to earn after one, two, or three or more years? Benefits can also add a lot to your base pay, but they vary widely. Find out exactly what the benefit package includes and how much of the cost you must bear for, say, medical or life insurance.

Finally, there will be an end to the job search process. You will be offered a position that meets your wants and needs, and you will accept it. Chapter

6 details what happens after you being work, helping you to maximize your potential for success in your new career.

THE INSIDE TRACK

Who:	Ray Cavallo
What:	Assistant Restaurant Manager
Where:	Coconuts Tropical Bar and Grill
	Milwaukee, Wisconsin

INSIDER'S STORY

I'm the assistant manager of a 100-seat restaurant and bar. I've been in this position for about a year, and I hope to take over as manager when the current manager leaves her position next year to open another store in the franchise. I started here as a host when I was in college. I had some part-time food service experience working in a sandwich shop, but I never had formal training as a restaurant manager. I studied business in college, and I think that experience has been helpful. The restaurant I worked for allowed me to work my way up from hosting to waiting tables, and then to being a shift supervisor, working under an assistant manager. Most of the managers at other restaurants in the franchise have been through a restaurant management program, and it definitely gives them an edge, combined with real-life experience, as they break into the field.

My primary function as assistant manager is to oversee the service that our customers receive. This encompasses a lot of things—supervising a staff of hosts, servers, and buspeople; creating work schedules; helping to hire servers and kitchen staff; and keeping up with practical aspects of the business, like the needs for recycling, kitchen supplies, and extermination, so that everything operates efficiently. I also close out the cash registers at the end of the day, balance the money against our sales records, and drop deposits at the bank—especially on the weekends when the general manager isn't working. At Coconuts, we do a lot of special events and theme nights, like singles' parties and weekly luau nights, and I do most of the coordination for those events too, including publicity, extra staffing needs, special supplies, and just making sure that our customers feel welcome and enjoy themselves.

When I become manager, I'll have some additional responsibilities, like monitoring the food we produce and serve. Since the restaurant I work in is part of a chain, another part of the manager's job is to keep up with new developments at the corporate level, and to make sure that the level of quality and service in our restaurant is in keeping with what our customers, and the corporate office, expect.

I find my work really satisfying. It's always a lot to juggle, and I think it takes a very organized person to perform well in this career. A lot of people are overwhelmed by how many different areas a job in management encompasses; you have to be able to keep tabs on all the aspects of the business. My advice to people entering the field would be to remember that even in a management position, your job will involve a lot of customer service. It's essential to know how to get along with other people—whether they're your employees or your customers—and always be diplomatic and tactful.

CHAPTER six

SUCCEEDING ON THE JOB

IN THIS CHAPTER, you will learn how to succeed once you have landed a job as a hotel or restaurant manager. You will find out how to fit in at your new work environment, whether you are employed at a large hotel, resort establishment, chain restaurant, or other work setting. We will also discuss forming positive relationships with the people you work with and dealing with stress on the job. Finally, a number of other ways in which you can put your career on the fast track, from dealing effectively with stress to handling criticism professionally, will be examined.

NOW THAT you are employed in your chosen profession, succeeding on the job is your next goal. You already have a understanding of a hotel or restaurant manager's basic duties and how to perform them, but your training didn't cover how to manage work relationships, or how to acclimate yourself to a new work environment. Even the valuable lessons learned during an internship aren't enough to prepare you completely for your new career. There is much to discover regarding how to perform well on the job, beyond what you were taught in the classroom. Read on to explore many of these topics, including finding and learning from a mentor, managing your time effectively, and getting along with your boss, so that you will be armed with the knowledge you need to succeed.

FITTING INTO THE WORKPLACE CULTURE

As a hotel or restaurant manager, you may find employment with any number of types of businesses, from international corporations to casinos, institutions, and small family-owned operations. Obviously, the workplace cultures of these employers vary greatly. Even among large companies you will find great differences; one may be formal and stiff, another is relaxed and casual, and yet another lies somewhere in between.

For managers, especially those who have been hired from another company, learning about the way things are done in their new environment can be tricky. In your position, you have a responsibility to set the tone and lead your "troops," and yet, in an established business, there already is a highly developed workplace culture. How do you learn how things are done in your hotel or restaurant, and at the same time, maintain a position of authority?

Begin by being attuned to the environment, intent on learning as much as you can as quickly as you can. This should be a primary goal during your first weeks and months on the job; once you gain an understanding of the workplace culture, it will help you to succeed in your new career by knowing what is expected of you, and what you can expect in return.

Whether you work in a small hotel or a corporate dining room, spend time observing and imitating. If you are working with other managers, or are in frequent contact with upper management, pay careful attention to the work habits of these coworkers, and follow suit. For instance, if management has lunch at a deli around the corner from your hotel every day, do the same. If the employees at your restaurant get to work 15 minutes early to have coffee together, make it a point to be there, too. After some time has passed, you will know better which customs and traditions are worth following and which you can deviate from. Next, a number of workplace customs found in the traditional corporate world, as well as those in less formal work settings, will be examined.

The corporate culture is becoming more and more the norm of the hospitality industry. Just a handful of large corporations own the majority of lodging establishments and casual dining restaurants in the country. This culture relies on a reporting structure and hierarchy to accomplish defined goals. Many large companies adopt this style simply because they have so many people to deal with. One manager (or president or vice president) cannot talk to everyone in the company all the time about their ideas. Instead, there is a functional reporting system. You might have a general manager, who has three senior managers, who have seven managers, one of whom is you.

For employees, the advantage in this type of culture is usually security—job security, the availability of additional training (often company paid), and a good, long-term salary with stock options and other perquisites. The disadvantage is that employees do not have as much freedom as in other places of employment and may have to spend more time on bureaucratic tasks, such as writing reports and filling out forms, than do those in other workplace cultures.

In a highly corporate culture, job titles are clearly defined, there is a predefined path to follow for raises and promotions, and there is little opportunity for an employee to shine outside of his or her own defined job. For instance, if you are hired as a sales manager, you won't have anything to do with catering or food service. Likewise, if you are hired to run the restaurant, you may have no say in how your establishment is marketed, or even staffed. Those decisions are made by other managers who may not even work in your city.

There are also opportunities for hotel or restaurant managers in less conservative, more casual work environments, as discussed in detail in Chapter 1. In settings like these, jeans and a sweater may be appropriate attire. Employers expect managers to work independently, and may encourage them to leave tradition behind in pursuit of new and better ways to get the job done. Even so, there are unwritten rules that govern this type of workplace culture. As with employment at a large company, you will need to pay careful attention in your first few weeks on the job. You will want to project an image of competence and authority, while observing the workplace and gaining a good working knowledge of the culture.

More casual settings, such as those in privately owned small hotels or restaurants, afford great possibilities to managers. First, you will be expected to wear many hats, and take responsibility for a wide range of tasks. For instance, the manager of a 50-room inn located in a resort town may need to hire and train employees, work closely with a bookkeeper, order supplies, spend time at the front desk, and develop a marketing plan for the inn. A restaurant manager in an independent restaurant may expect the same type of diverse workload.

The downside of working in a non-corporate environment is that your employer doesn't have the resources of a large company to support the business. Your salary will probably be lower than that of a peer working for a corporation, and you may never see perks such as a pension plan, comprehensive medical insurance, and stock options. If you are working for someone new to the business, you may have to deal with the instability that comes with not knowing if you will have a job in the near future; the hospitality industry is very competitive, and typically only those who show a profit will stay in business.

No matter where you begin working, you may find that after your first week on the job that you don't fit into the workplace culture. While first impressions are important, you should plan to spend some time in your new position before deciding for certain that it isn't working. As mentioned earlier, it takes time to understand an environment and learn all of its unwritten rules. Give yourself a number of weeks or even months to fully integrate yourself into the culture of your new workplace.

MANAGING WORK RELATIONSHIPS

The management circle of the hospitality industry is a tight-knit community. While early in your career you might not feel a connection with another manager who is 3,000 miles away, you will soon find you have much in common. You may order supplies from the same companies, recruit new employees at the same job fairs or college campuses, or share the same upper management team. The point is, the circle is connected, and once you become a part of it, you will want to form positive business relationships with every person you come across.

In fact, your success as a hotel or restaurant manager will depend in large part on the relationships you develop and cultivate. Making a conscious effort to respect others while on the job will help your career immensely. In your current position, you will gain the respect of those you work with daily. And when you are ready to move on to a higher-level position, these relationships will aid you in networking your way up.

Basic Rules

When it comes to building and maintaining professional relationships, some basic rules apply to any workplace.

1. **Sometimes peace is better than justice.**

   You may be absolutely, 100% sure you are right about a specific situation. Unfortunately, you may have employees or superiors who doubt you or who flatly disagree with you. This is a common occurrence in the workplace.

   In some situations, you need to assert your position and convince the disbelievers to trust your judgment. Your previous track record and reputation will go a long way in helping to convince people to trust your opinions, ideas, and decisions. However, carefully consider the gravity of the situation before you stick your neck out.

   In other words, in a work environment, choose your battles wisely. For instance, go ahead and argue your position if you can prevent a catastrophe, or if your leadership role demands it. On the other hand, if you are having a debate about an issue of taste, opinion, or preference with your superiors, it is advisable to leave the situation alone or accept their decisions. It may be appropriate to let your recommendation(s) be known, but do not argue your point relentlessly. Sometimes you will be right and people will not listen to you. Always be open to compromise and be willing to listen to and consider the options and ideas of others.

   In terms of guests, peace is almost always better than justice. Your employer will cover this topic during training, but it is worth repeating here. The company's bottom line depends on returning customers. It is your job to make certain they leave satisfied, every time. The very few exceptions occur when a guest is abusive or his words and/or actions are completely inappropriate. However, it is still your job to maintain your composure and handle the situation as peacefully as possible.

2. **Don't burn bridges.**

   If you are in a disagreement, or if you are leaving one employment situation for another, always leave the work relationship on a good note. Keep in mind that your professional reputation will follow you throughout your career. It will take years to build a positive reputation, but only one mistake could destroy it.

When changing jobs, don't take the opportunity to vent negative thoughts and feelings before you leave. While it might make you feel good in the short term, it will have a detrimental, lasting effect on your career and on people's perception of you. Someone you argued with could become your boss someday or be in a position to help you down the line.

If you wind up acting unprofessionally toward someone, even if you don't ever have contact with that person again, he or she will have contact with many other people and possibly describe you as hard to work with or rude. Your work reputation is very important; don't tarnish it by burning your bridges.

3. **Keep your work and social lives separate.**

You were hired to do a job, not to meet new friends and potential dates. Although the hospitality industry, because of its unconventional hours and teamwork atmosphere, has a reputation for on-the-job romance, there are great risks to getting involved with a coworker. It is important to be friendly and form positive relationships with the people you work with while maintaining a professional attitude. Personal relationships can interfere with your job performance, and your job performance can weaken or destroy a friendship, especially if you are working directly with or for a friend.

The challenges associated with at-work romances can lead to disaster. Not only could you endanger your ability to do your job, but you may also set yourself up for unemployment. There are many employers who frown upon office romances, and some that have strict policies against them. If your coworkers find out about your relationship, depending upon where you work, you could end up looking for another job.

Your Boss

An excellent relationship is a gift, a bad one a daily nightmare; most fall somewhere in between. Because no two bosses are alike, just as no two managers are alike, it is impossible to give advice that will cover every situation; however, there are a few rules that you can apply to this important relationship that will make it more rewarding and conflict-free. Following are some suggestions to help you start building a cooperative relationship with your boss, providing he or she is rational and motivated in that direction.

▶ **Be as clear as possible about what your boss expects.**

If you don't have a formal, written job description and you feel even minimally comfortable asking for one, do so. It takes some tact to do this; you should start by explaining why you want one. Don't say, "I would like my job description in writing, please." That sounds like a challenge, or as though you are opposed to doing anything that is not in the description. It is best to say something like, "If possible, I would like to get a list of the duties I will be performing every day. I know it is not possible to describe everything, but I don't want to leave anything undone that I am responsible for." Ask for this information at the very beginning of your relationship, before any tension has built up, so it won't seem like a challenge to your boss's authority.

▶ **If you don't understand your boss's instructions, ask for clarification.**

You cannot work effectively if you don't know what is expected of you. If instructions for doing a task are unclear, you must ask for further details. Don't be afraid of appearing stupid. Most bosses would prefer that you ask for clarification rather than try to muddle through and make mistakes.

▶ **Be flexible.**

If your boss occasionally asks you to do something that is not in your job description—as long as the demand isn't unethical (dishonest or sexist, for example)—it is best to go ahead and do it. If you are rigid about what you will and won't do, your boss is liable to become rigid too. If she or he consistently expects you to perform tasks outside your job description—things you feel are demeaning, especially—

eventually you will have to say, very diplomatically, that you are not comfortable doing them.

▶ **Make your boss look good.**

This could go under the heading of "office politics." You don't have to think hard to see why it makes sense to do whatever you can to enhance your superior's image. Two important reasons are that upper management will make the decisions about how far you will get in your career with their company, and your success goes hand-in-hand with the success of the company. The person or persons responsible for promoting you (or denying you promotions), and generally making your day-to-day routine pleasant or miserable, will respond positively to your efforts to make him or her look good. By adding positive energy to upper management, you help the whole team, which can translate into a better business. And, if the company is doing well, they will have more to offer you in terms of salary, benefits, and opportunities for better positions.

▶ **Don't go over your boss's head except for the most dire reasons.**

It is not an inviolable rule never to complain about your boss to a higher authority. In cases of actual discrimination or harassment, you should go to someone else. But in general, it is best to take complaints to your boss first and try to settle the matter privately—give him or her a chance to correct bad behavior or explain policies that seem unreasonable or unclear. This takes courage, but the payoffs are large. You may find there is a reason behind your boss's "unreasonable" behavior that you never thought of.

▶ **Understand that your boss has problems too.**

When someone has authority over you, it may be hard to remember that they are just human. They have kids at home who misbehave, cats that need to go to the vet, deadlines to meet, and bosses of their own—sometimes difficult ones—overseeing their work. If your boss occasionally acts unreasonable, don't take it personally, as it might have nothing to do with you. Of course, if his or her behavior is consistently abusive, you will have to do something about it. But occasional mood swings are something we are all entitled to.

The best way to handle demands that aren't horrendous but only annoying—failure to make priorities clear, for example—is to ask your boss for a one-on-one conference to clarify things. If you keep focused during the conference on the needs of the team, it will probably go smoothly, and your work life will be more pleasant and rewarding.

Your Employees

During training for your new position, you were educated in the management style of your employer. But while directing and supervising your employees, you will undoubtedly come across some who add to the team and get their jobs done, but create problems for you. The important things to concentrate on are your job performance, and the needs of the team. This attitude will help keep you focused and will lessen the impact of the inevitable interpersonal tensions that are part of work life. Remember the rules of good ethics, which apply to every situation:

► **Take responsibility for your actions.**

   Don't blame the company, your boss, or your employees for your mistakes. When you are the one in the wrong, own up to it. In a well-run organization, it is not fatal to admit you have made an error. Conversely, don't grovel or say you are wrong when you don't believe you are.

► **Never take credit for another's ideas.**

   Not only is it wrong, but chances are that eventually you will be found out.

► **Do not violate confidentiality, whether the company's or an employee's.**

   As a hotel or restaurant manager, you will likely be privy to company or organization information that is confidential. Similarly, you will, in a position of authority, be trusted with personal confidences. Although you may be tempted, do not violate confidentiality in either case, as you can seriously damage the company or organization for which you work, or your work relationships.

▶ **Refuse to cover up serious wrongdoing.**

While violating legitimate confidentiality is always ill-advised, neither should you cover up serious violations of ethics, whether by employees, your boss, or even the company or organization itself. "I was just doing my job" is not an acceptable excuse for ethics violations anymore. If you find yourself working for a boss or company with ethics that seriously violate yours, never use the excuse "I am just a manager." Even if you can't bring yourself to blow the whistle (which may be the right thing to do, but can have horrible consequences), at least start looking for another job.

▶ **Help others, especially new employees.**

You need to provide support for your staff if you want to keep turnover to a minimum. This doesn't mean making excuses for them, or allowing them to perform at less than professional levels. It does mean showing that you are part of the team, too. In particular, give new employees extra support. We are all familiar with that sweaty-palmed feeling of the first day of work, even the first weeks of work. Remember what it is like to be new, and empathize.

▶ **Be positive about others' achievements.**

Never undermine anyone in your establishment by devaluing their achievements, even if their "achievements" seem minor. Don't be afraid that another person will look better than you. In a good work-place, one in which teamwork is valued, there is room for everyone to look good.

▶ **Do not complain to the boss about a coworker's behavior.**

This is unacceptable, unless the matter is extremely serious. Even if the behavior of a coworker is really egregious, try every other avenue to resolve the situation before complaining to your boss. If a coworker is committing infractions that violate important ethical rules (consistent sexist or racist treatment of other employees would be an example) or that violate confidentiality or otherwise damage the company or its customers, of course a complaint is in order. But for lesser matters—especially for interpersonal conflicts—complaints to the boss, reminiscent of tattling in grade school, have a way of backfiring. It is best to talk to the person involved, or, if it is something minor, simply to ignore the behavior.

▶ **Don't engage in gossip.**

Gossip hurts the person being talked about, will inevitably come back to haunt you, and also can make you look like you don't have enough to do.

▶ **When conflicts arise, attack the problem, not the other person.**

If the bookkeeper is consistently late getting invoices to you, making you work late, talk to him or her when you can remain calm and focused. Keep the discussion centered on how the problem affects your life and work, not on how terrible the other person is. Just as you would with your boss, ask for a one-on-one conference, and keep the good of the team uppermost in your mind.

Instead of saying, "It is your responsibility to see that invoices get to me on time. How am I supposed to do my job, anyway? From now on, do it right," say something like, "Could we work something out about the timing of the invoice delivery? If I get them at the last minute, I don't have time to contact the suppliers if I need to make changes." If the other person ignores your request, repeat it at intervals. Chances are you will wear him or her down, or your boss will notice the bad behavior and do something about it.

STRESS ON THE JOB

According to the American Institute of Stress, job stress is estimated to cost U.S. industry $300 billion annually, because of absenteeism, diminished productivity, employee turnover, and direct medical, legal, and insurance fees. As a manager, you will want to do all you can to handle stress well, for both yourself and your employees, before it leads to these types of problems. Let's first look at the kinds of stress experienced in the hospitality industry, and then examine some proven methods for dealing with them.

What You Can Expect

There can be an incredible amount of stress associated with work in hotels and restaurants. Not only will you have to contend with long hours and work on nights, weekends, and holidays, but you may be confronted with irate guests, employees who don't show up for work or who perform at less than optimal levels, supplies that aren't delivered on time, or large groups of tourists or convention attendees who need coordinating of a variety of services. As Darby Crum, a managing partner of a large restaurant corporation, who began as a management trainee, puts it:

> One of the stresses of my job is knowing that the doors will open on time, no matter what. I may be short-staffed, or a piece of equipment may be broken, but people will come to my restaurant expecting me to greet them with a smile and not have to know what I am going through. My guests are not window shopping; once they are in the restaurant, they have committed to buying, and have high expectations about the product.

The hotel business is much the same: Guests will arrive expecting their room to be ready, and service to be impeccable, no matter what kinds of problems your establishment is experiencing. You will need to remain calm and get the job done, all with a smile, while confronting issues involving employees, equipment, supplies, even the weather.

Because hotel are open 24 hours a day, 365 days a year, and restaurants are open on nights, weekends, and holidays, the workweek of a manager is usually long. The Bureau of Labor Statistics reports that restaurant and hotel managers are often on the job more than 60 hours a week. These hours can lead to fatigue, which can lead to stress. They can also cause friction within a family, as discussed in greater detail in the next section.

As a manager, you will need to address the impact of stress on your employees as well. Their stress levels can cause poor performance, which has a direct impact on your bottom line. A survey done by Zagat Survey LLC in 40 different markets concluded that while training and service have improved over the years, 50% of reported customer complaints relate to service and only 15% relate to food. If a guest finds the waitstaff to be rude, the silverware dirty, or the wait for a table too long, they won't likely be back to your restaurant, with competition as fierce as it is in most markets.

Stressed-out employees are also more likely to leave their jobs. Although the American Institute of Stress reports that 40% of worker turnover is due to stress, this figure represents the American workforce as a whole. In the hospitality industry, stress is often cited as the number one reason for the high turnover rate. A study of 229 full service hotels from ten hotel companies conducted by the Educational Institute (EI), the American Hotel & Motel Association (AH&MA), and KPMG Peat Marwick, found annual employee turnover rates to be 158% for line-level employees. The picture in restaurants is similar; a recent article in the Nation's Restaurant News (www.nrn.com) reports that a study of 200 restaurant chains concluded they were losing $3.4 billion dollars annually on employee turnover.

In addition to the stresses you will come face-to-face with on a daily basis are the stresses imposed upon hotel and restaurant managers from upper management who want to maximize their profits. Most companies in the hospitality industry operate on a small profit percentage, meaning that, for every sale, most of the money must go to built-in costs such as salaries, facilities, supplies, et cetera. In order to succeed, these companies must rely on quantity or a large number of sales (dinners ordered, rooms reserved).

Upper management will be greatly concerned with maximizing their small profit percentage and eliminating avoidable mistakes, which lead to waste and diminished profits. Therefore, you will be expected to run your establishment with one eye constantly on the bottom line. Food waste, rooms that are left empty, catering halls that aren't rented all lead to lower profits, and more pressure on you to stay on budget and make money for your employers.

Dealing with Stress

There are varying degrees to which people respond to stress. While in school, you probably noticed that some students sailed through exams, while others became anxious, unable to eat or sleep adequately. The same holds true for on-the-job stress. You will find some managers with short fuses who blow up and create a scene over just about any minor problem. Others face obstacles with a clear head and calmly find solutions. While some of these variations may be blamed on personality types, the truth is there is much you can do to reduce the impact of stressful job situations.

Individual factors, such as physical health and the quality of your support system, greatly influence your ability to deal with stress. Getting adequate rest, eating well-balanced meals, and having close friends with whom you can vent your frustrations and share your accomplishments all contribute to your overall well-being and make you better able to handle the stresses inherent with your position as manager.

Graham Harris, in an article on the Hotel Resource website (www. hotelresource.com), shows that another effective way to deal with on-the-job stress, especially that caused by angry customers or superiors, is to change the way you think and feel about it. Harris notes that you decide to allow yourself to be stressed by others' behavior when you internalize it, believing you have done something wrong. By seeing the angry person as someone performing a role, in which anger is a necessary part, you distance yourself from the behavior. If you are confronted by an irate guest, say to yourself, "This guest is playing the role of an angry person—his performance is fantastic!" When you are not allowing the behavior to cause you stress, you can then calmly observe the angry person and react rationally, often finding a solution to the problem that you wouldn't have thought of had you been stressed out.

Many of the stresses involving employees and guest relations are directly related to how well you train and reward those who work for you. Employees who feel they are undervalued and are made to work long shifts are prone to stress, and thus to leaving their jobs, leaving you with a high turnover rate. The solution isn't simple. Vivienne Wildes, director of the National Waiters Association, conducted a Pennsylvania State survey of 6,000 restaurant guests, and concludes:

> Put waiters in a 401(k) plan, give them medical and dental benefits, and launder their uniforms, and you will see a significant improvement in attracting and retaining quality servers.

However, your employer may not be willing to consider such incentives. It then falls to you as a manager, to do all you can to keep your employees satisfied and feeling valued. That means building relationships with them as individuals. If they are consistently asked to work on weekends and holidays, and then feel pressure from their families because of it, they won't perform well on the job and may look for employment elsewhere. Michele Bailey DiMartino, vice president and director of EI's Center for Hospitality Research Solutions, notes:

> Employers must take into consideration what is happening at home, and realize that in order to keep valued employees, they must develop and support the whole person—not just the man or woman who shows up as the front desk clerk each day. Employers don't like to hear this, and, granted, it is not an easy area of employee relations and development to affect. However, it is necessary in order to retain some of our better performers.

Spend time with those working for you and get to know them. You might find that one or more of them are interested in a career in your profession, giving you the opportunity to be a mentor. Even if they look at their employment as "just a job," your showing care and consideration may make them want to stick with it for much longer than they would have if they felt that their work environment was cold and unresponsive to their needs.

MANAGING YOUR TIME

Good time management is an important aspect of any hotel or restaurant manager job. Being able to know what needs to be done when and having the work habits necessary for getting it all done well and on time are crucial to your success. In addition, good time management skills help to reduce stress, as you won't be constantly "surprised" by deadlines you should have remembered, and have to work longer hours to complete tasks that shouldn't take so much of your time.

Daily Work Activities

Practicing good habits when dealing with your daily work activities is essential. Hotel and restaurant managers are expected to perform a variety of tasks, many during the same time period. In order to keep things moving smoothly, remember the following:

1. **Know the requirements of your job and what is expected of you.**

   Define your role and know what you are expected to deliver on a daily basis. If you have an assistant manager, make sure he or she understands that role, and don't take on their tasks yourself.

2. **Don't get trapped by interruptions and time wasters.**

   Every job is subject to time wasters. Some get caught up in chatting with employees; others spend too much time playing with their personal digital assistants (PDAs). Although it is important to allow a small amount of relaxation throughout the day, set limits for yourself, so it doesn't get out of control. E-mail and voice mail can become major time wasters and distractions. Set aside specific times during the day (time management experts recommend no more than three times) to listen to or read messages and answer those requiring you to do so. This is especially important during the time you set aside for paperwork, ordering of supplies, bookkeeping, and other "back room" tasks. The more interruptions you get, the longer it will take to get even the simplest things done.

3. **Keep a day planner.**

   Identify one place where you write (or type) everything down, whether it is a daily planner, personal digital assistant (PDA), or specialized scheduling software for your computer. This is the number one "secret" of those who get nearly everything on their to-do list done, when it needs to be done. It is not that these people have better memories than yours; they are just better organized and can find the information they need at a glance because they keep it all in one place.

4. **Do a small amount of organization when you arrive at work each morning.**

   Look at your planner and make any small revisions as needed. From the tasks on your agenda, make a to-do list for the day. Make sure that tasks contributing to long-term goals get on the list; the goals won't be reached unless you spend time working toward them. While each day can bring new challenges and unforeseen obstacles, if you have your to-do list taken care of, you will have more time and energy to deal with the crises.

Improving Time Management Skills

If you find that this is an area in which you can improve, begin to do so immediately. Learning time management skills won't add more hours to the work day, but it will allow you to use all of your time more productively, reduce the stress in your life, better focus on what is important, and ultimately get more done faster. If you have decided to use a time management tool such as a computer program or personal digital assistant, spend the time necessary to learn how to use it properly. These tools are only as effective as their user, and although it may take a large time investment to get started, it will be well worth it.

Next, over the course of several days, analyze how you spend every minute of your day. Determine what takes up the majority of your time but diminishes your productivity. Perhaps you experience countless interruptions such as long telephone calls from upper management, you don't have well-defined priorities, your work area is messy and disorganized, or you have too much to do and become overwhelmed. As you examine how you spend your day, pinpoint the biggest time wasters that are keeping you from getting your most important work done.

Take major projects, goals, and objectives and divide them into smaller, more manageable tasks. You will need to incorporate your to-do list into your daily planner, allowing you to schedule your time and record that schedule where you will be able to refer to it often. Make sure you attempt to complete your high-priority items and tasks when you experience the fewest interruptions, giving those items your full attention. Also, make sure you list all of your pre-scheduled appointments in your daily schedule, allowing ample time to get to and from the appointments, and if necessary, prepare for them in advance.

Once you commit to using a time management tool, it is important to remain disciplined, using it continuously until it becomes second nature. Initially, you may have to spend up to 30 minutes per day planning your time and creating your to-do list, but ultimately, you will begin saving up to several hours per day. Learning to better manage your time will boost your productivity, which will ultimately make you more valuable to an employer, putting you in a better position to receive a raise or promotion.

MENTORS

Finding and learning from a mentor is probably one of the best ways to continue your education on the job, providing you with both a positive role model to learn from and a professional "coach," someone who sees your job performance and knows ways in which you can improve upon it. A mentor can give you the kind of insider information not covered during your training and help you develop a path for your career.

Finding a Mentor

You will probably need to actively search for a mentor, unless someone decides to take you under his or her wing and show you the ropes. A mentor can be anyone from another manager, to a supplier, or a superior. There is no formula for who makes a good mentor; title, level of seniority, or years in the field may be unimportant. Instead, the qualities of a good mentor are based on a combination of willingness to mentor, level of expertise in a certain area, teaching ability, and attitude.

Look for a mentor by getting involved in an alumni group, or professional society. Attend conferences, and ask for the e-mail addresses of those who you think may be good mentor candidates. Follow up by corresponding, and be frank about your interest in the person as a mentor. A recent article in *Restaurants and Institutions Magazine* tells the story of how Kathy Granquist, director of operations at Dallas-based T.G.I. Friday's, met her mentor, Hala Moddelmog, president of Atlanta-based Church's Chicken (and one of the highest ranking women in food service), through the Women's

Foodservice Forum. Granquist felt so positively about her experience with a mentor that she started an informal in-house mentoring program for 12 of her general managers.

In addition to professional associations and groups, you might also find a mentor at work. When looking within your place of employment, seek counsel from three kinds of mentors:

1. a "higher up" (but not your boss, or you might be accused of simply currying favor) who can give you informal soundings on what your superiors think of your work

2. a peer from another area of your place of employment, who can teach you about aspects of the company or organization you do not yet know

3. an employee, who can tell you what your "troops" think of your supervisory style

When looking for a mentor, keep in mind the following questions:

▶ Who in your company/group/association has a great reputation as a true professional?

▶ Does the potential mentor tackle problems in a reasonable manner until they are resolved?

▶ What is it that people admire about the potential mentor? Do the admirable qualities coincide with your values and goals?

▶ Is he or she strong in areas that you are weak?

If you think you have found a mentor at work, spend time watching that person on the job. You can learn a lot about him or her through observation. When asked a question, does he or she take the time to help you find the solution, or does he or she point you toward someone else who can help you? The one who takes the time to help you resolve your question is the better choice for a mentor. Observe your potential mentor when he or she is working on a problem. Does he or she do so in a calm manner? Does the problem get resolved? If so, you may have found a good mentor.

Learning From a Mentor

Once you have entered into a mentoring relationship, intend to learn all you can. While there are no set rules about what a mentor can teach you, there are some specifics that are part of the "curriculum" in many mentoring relationships. The following is a list of things you may learn from a mentor:

▶ coworker interaction skills
▶ what to expect in your work environment
▶ how to communicate with the chain of command in your company
▶ in-depth knowledge about the technology used by your company
▶ the best hospitality industry magazines, websites, and other resource material
▶ how best to advance in your career
▶ what conferences/classes/training programs you should attend
▶ advice on dealing with difficult guests or customers

Once you find someone who seems to be the ideal mentor, don't feel compelled to stick with him or her forever. Career growth may open up possibilities to you in new areas of specialization. If that happens, you will probably want to find additional mentors who can show you the ropes in the new environment. However, maintain relationships with former mentors—as previously discussed, the hospitality industry is a close community, and the more allies you have, the easier it will be to succeed and advance in your career.

PROMOTING YOURSELF

There are a number of other things you can do to keep your career moving in a positive direction. Don't wait for opportunities to land in your lap. Rather, you should create them by being proactive; promote yourself in your current position, and/or seek out a promotion to a higher-level job.

Building on Your Reputation

No matter how well you work with others and how organized you are, in the end you will be judged by the product you put out. You want to develop a reputation as someone who gets the job done, correctly, and on time. To accomplish this, make sure you know exactly what is expected of you. It doesn't hurt to ask for clarification if you are unsure about how to proceed. Take pride in everything you do, and do it to the best of your ability.

Perhaps most importantly, work toward increasing your abilities. You might decide to attend a seminar on a specialized topic in management. Or, you could join a lodging or food service association (see Appendix A for a listing of many associations, with contact information), and get involved at a local level. Make it a point to visit informative websites such as www. restaurantreport.com, which contain articles on new management techniques, industry trends, and updates in the field. Read one or more of the trade journals, listed in the following box, on a regular basis. Actively pursue knowledge, experience, and greater involvement in your career, and in the industry in which you work.

Hospitality Industry Trade Journals and Magazines

Restaurant

Nation's Restaurant News
425 Park Avenue
New York, NY 10022
www.nrn.com

Restaurants and Institutions Magazine
1350 East Touhy Avenue
P.O. Box 5080
Des Plaines, IL 60017-5080
www.rimag.com

Restaurants USA
National Restaurant Association
1200 17th Street NW
Washington, DC 20036
www.restaurant.org/rusa

Hotel

Hotel & Motel Management
131 West First Street
Duluth, MN 55802
www.hotelmotel.com

Hotels Magazine
1350 E. Touhy Avenue
Des Plaines, IL 60018
www.hotelsmag.com

Lodging Magazine
1707 L Street NW, Suite 200
Washington, DC 20036
www.lodgingnews.com

Hospitality

CHRIE Communique (newsletter)
International Council On Hotel,
   Restaurant & Institutional
   Education
3205 Skipwith Road
Richmond, VA 23294-4442

*Cornell Hotel and Restaurant
   Administration Quarterly (HRAQ)*
School of Hotel Administration
Statler Hall
Cornell University
Ithaca, NY 14853
www.hotelschool.cornell.edu/
   publications/hraq

*Hosteur Webzine For Future
   Hospitality & Tourism Professionals*
www.chrie.org/public/publications/
   hosteur/hosteur.html

Hospitality Review
Florida International University
School of Hospitality
North Miami, FL 33181
www.fiu.edu/~review

NEWH Magazine
Network of Executive Women in
   Hospitality, Inc.
PO Box 322
Shawano, WI 54166
www.newh.org

Dealing Positively With Criticism

When you do receive criticism about your job performance from a colleague or superior, you need to do three things. The first is to remain calm. You need to hear what is being said, and that is nearly impossible when you are upset. Listen and understand without trying to defend yourself or correcting the person who is critiquing your work.

Second, ask for clarification and concrete help to rectify the situation. If you have been told that the employee schedules you devised were unsatisfactory, find out exactly what the problem was. Does your boss prefer that you use another scheduling software package, or would she like you to consider more employee scheduling requests? Ask for specific information in a nonconfrontational way.

Third, follow any advice given, and ask the person who's critiquing you for help in the future. See if you can find a time when he or she can see how you have been doing things and make specific suggestions for changes. By keeping calm, and responding in a non-defensive, professional manner, you can turn a negative critique into an opportunity for positive growth and change.

Getting Promoted

Once you have been on the job for a while, you may decide that the position you hold isn't as challenging or rewarding as it once was. If you work in a large company, there may be promotion opportunities to seek out. Entry-level management jobs can lead to higher-level positions with more responsibility, greater visibility, and better pay.

If you decide you would like to seek a promotion, either immediately or in the future, prepare well by taking four critical steps. If you plan well and think in terms of your career as a whole rather than just your first position in the industry, you will prepare for your rise through the ranks as soon as you land a job. The people who get promoted are those who:

1. know their company
2. maintain a positive attitude toward change
3. show genuine care for guests and employees
4. get to know upper management

The first step may take some time, but it is probably the easiest. You will need to become extremely well versed in your company's mission statement, philosophies, history, financial statements, operating procedures, training procedures, and job duties. Much of this information will be presented during your training and first weeks on the job. Pay close attention, and really get to know and understand what your employer is all about. You will sound more authoritative when speaking about your company, and operate from a knowledgeable position.

Second, embrace the changes that will inevitably become a part of your "routine." The hospitality industry is very sensitive to trends, and therefore change is frequent. Large-scale trends include the economy, which plays a big part in the decision-making process for hotels and restaurants. For instance, in a slow economy or recession, people will travel less, and spend less when they do travel. They may not frequent restaurants as often as they do in better times. Hotels and restaurants respond, for example, by offering lower priced items on their menus, and promoting quick weekend "getaways" close to home with an all-inclusive low rate.

Smaller scale trends include the (often fleeting) popularity of specific food and beverage choices. When news emerges, for example, about the health benefits of a diet that includes more protein and fewer carbohydrates, the food service industry responds by incorporating menu items that reflect the trend. If a survey indicates that a particular wine is growing in popularity, smart managers will feature it in their establishments.

Another trend may find people choosing to eat at home rather than in a restaurant; many restaurants now offer meals "to go" in response. When upper management responds to such trends by changing operational procedures, you need to be positive. Let your superiors know you will do all you can to support the new procedure(s), contributing to its success. Change is the operative word in the industry; those who embrace it, and use it to increase sales, will probably be the ones who succeed.

Another attitude-oriented step is showing a genuine care and concern for others. Restaurant manager Darby Crum notes that, in order to do this consistently, you need a "game face" when on the job.

> Even though you show up for work on some days feeling blah, no one should ever know it. Put on a game face that is positive and outgoing; show care for people no matter what kind of day you are having. You need to make both guests and employees feel that they're important.

Finally, if you want to get promoted, you need to know upper management. When you meet them, make a great impression. Discover ways to help them remember you, and play the politics of your company. It may take some time to understand how the game is played, but make it a priority to observe it at all times. Find out how those in upper management were promoted, and why. Keep an ear open to inside information and gossip. Frequent your company's website and promotional material for other clues.

When it comes time to ask or apply for a promotion, be sure to understand your company's protocol. If applying in person, don't aggressively demand the job, but be prepared to explain why you are right for it. Your enthusiasm and confidence will show if you have researched the job, know you have the necessary skills, and are excited about taking on the extra responsibility. If you need to apply in writing, use the same care as if you were applying for your first position in the company. Update your resume to include your current job, pointing out the skills and responsibilities you possess that are needed for the new position.

Try to keep the application process low key. There is a possibility you won't get the promotion this time around, for any number of reasons. You don't want to hurt your chances in the future by exhibiting unprofessional behavior, such as complaining about not getting the job. You are still employed, and still have a job to do for your company. Spend some time quietly figuring out why you weren't promoted; keep your ears open for any news about who did get the job and why. If it is appropriate, ask the person making the hiring decision for information about his or her choice. If there is something you can do to improve your chances in the future, begin to take steps to do so now.

MOVING ON

Suppose you decide, after several years (or even months), that your new job isn't all you thought it would be. Or suppose it is, but now you have gained so much skill and knowledge that you have outgrown the position and/or the company you work for. The right career move in these circumstances is to look for a new job.

This is often the only avenue for promotion within the higher management ranks of the hospitality industry. There aren't endless levels of managers, so in order to advance or be promoted, you will probably need to change positions or change companies (waiting for a superior to move on, leaving a position open, is not the way most managers get ahead). If a restaurant manager has no direct position to which to be promoted (that may be the highest food service position in the restaurant), she may decide to become a sales manager, which brings a higher salary and better benefits in her company. A hotel manager is similarly situated; unless you are waiting for your boss to vacate his or her position, you will probably have to look for a position with another company to advance.

This could mean moving from a 50-room inn to a 500-room hotel, or leaving a manager's position at a chain restaurant for a large institutional catering facility. But whatever type of job change you are contemplating, be sure of your reasons. This is not the kind of move you should make often. Keep in mind that your resume will be read by every potential new employer, who will want to know why you left prior positions. If you list a number of jobs held over a short period of time, you may appear unreliable, difficult to get along with, or simply immature. But there are legitimate reasons for moving on, including the following:

▶ You have learned new skills or improved old ones to the point where your current job is no longer challenging.

▶ You like your job but don't find what your company or organization does very interesting.

▶ There's a specialized position you have discovered an interest in (for instance, employment with a cruise line, spa, or golf resort).

▶ You are moving to a new town.

▶ You dislike your job or the office atmosphere for any one of a variety of reasons (dull work, abusive boss, unethical business practices, or simply lack of anything meaningful in common with your coworkers).

▶ You are pretty sure the company you work for is downsizing, or you sense it is in financial trouble. Don't rely on gossip—make absolutely sure—but sometimes the signs are unmistakable.

Once you have decided that you have sound, legitimate reasons for moving on, maintain a professional attitude on the job (refer back to the "basic rules" concerning the need to avoid burning bridges). To maintain a good reputation within the industry, it is important to act appropriately right up to the last time you walk out the employer's door.

If the reason you are changing jobs is because of a difficult boss, a professional attitude is especially important. Getting into a fight with your boss, shouting, "I quit!" and then stomping out of the building forever is never the best way to handle things. Before alerting anyone about your impending resignation, begin searching for a new job. It is never a good idea to wait until after you have left one position to start looking for another. If there are any hard feelings on the part of your former employer, they could cause problems during a job search.

Once you have actually landed a new job, be prepared to give your current employer the traditional two weeks notice. Arrange a private meeting with your boss or with the appropriate person within the company, and offer your resignation in person, following it up in writing with a friendly and professional letter. Some people give notice and then use their accumulated vacation or sick days to avoid showing up for work. This is not appropriate behavior. Even if your new employer wants you to start work immediately, they will almost always understand that as a matter of loyalty and professional courtesy, it is necessary for you to stay with your current employer for those two weeks after giving your notice.

During those last two weeks on the job, offer to do whatever you can to maintain a positive relationship with your coworkers and boss, such as offering to train your replacement. Make your exit from the employer as smooth as possible. Purposely causing problems, stealing from the employer, or sabotaging business deals are all actions that are unethical and totally inappropriate. Some employers will request your immediate departure when you quit, especially if you are leaving on a negative note. Prior to quitting, try to determine how past coworkers were treated, so you will know what to expect.

As you actually leave the company for the last time, take with you only your personal belongings and nothing that is considered the company's property. Make a point to return, directly to your boss, your keys, and any company-owned equipment that was in your possession. If possible, for your protection, obtain a written memo stating that everything was returned promptly and in working order.

FINAL THOUGHTS

As we have noted throughout this book, the hiring outlook for hotel and restaurant managers is good, and doesn't appear likely to slow down in the future. Demand for those holding degrees in the hospitality industry is greatest; both lodging establishments and restaurants prefer to hire managers who have graduated from four-year programs. In order to stay competitive after you have been hired, don't let learning stop after graduation. Get involved in industry associations, attend conferences and seminars, and keep your knowledge current.

Not only are there always a large number of job openings, but hotel and restaurant management positions require great responsibility, increasing use of technology, and a wide range of career directions and specializations. Pursue each step toward your new career with diligence, perseverance, and a commitment to excellence, and you will be well on your way to achieving success.

THE INSIDE TRACK

Who:	Alisa Clevenger
What:	Hospitality Manager
Where:	High Tide Cruises
	Miami, FL

INSIDER'S STORY

I was never the type of person who wanted to work in an office all day. I got my A.A.S. degree in Tourism and Hospitality Management because I knew that it was a career that could take me places—literally! I am a Hospitality Manager on a cruise line that operates between Miami and a number of Caribbean islands. Generally, most of our cruises last between 7–10 days, but we also operate "weekend getaways" and cruises that last as long as six weeks.

Working on a cruise line is somewhat different than working in a hotel or resort, in that our guests are with us pretty much 24 hours a day. They will disembark from the ship for day trips, but for much of their stay, the ship serves as both their lodging and their primary source of entertainment. My job as hospitality manager is to ensure that they are comfortable and content. I supervise a staff of hospitality specialists; guests have access to our services all the time. In fact, I started as a hospitality specialist myself, and I was promoted to manager after a little more than a year. We can help guests with any number of things, from sending a fax to getting new linens for their cabin to simply finding something to do for the afternoon.

As hospitality manager, I communicate with other departments, like dining, house-keeping, and entertainment, and let them know about any challenges or problems our guests have let us know about. The hospitality staff is the group that has the most frequent interactions with our guests, so we get firsthand feedback about what they enjoy, as well as any suggestions they might have. I also collaborate with the entertainment staff to plan fun daytime activities, like casual sports and crafts workshops.

One of the most important qualities I look for in my staff is patience. It can be easy for our guests to get bored or irritable, since there are long periods when they're unable to leave the ship. As a staff, it doesn't do any good for us to respond with a similar attitude; instead, the hospitality staff needs to have compassion and remain upbeat. We try to remember that even if our own jobs may seem a little routine sometimes, every day is a unique experience for our guests. We want people to have the best vacation possible, and sometimes it's the little details that make that happen.

Appendix A

Professional Associations

American Hotel & Lodging Association
    (AH&LA)
1201 New York Avenue NW, #600
Washington, DC 20005-3931
Phone: 202-289-3100
Fax: 202-289-3199
www.ahla.com

Hospitality Sales & Marketing Association
    International (HSMAI)
1300 L Street NW, Suite 1020
Washington, DC 20005
Phone: 202-789-0089
Fax: 202-789-1725
www.hsmai.org

The American Society of Training and
    Development (ASTD)
1640 King Street, Box 1443
Alexandria, VA 22313-2043
Phone: 703-683-8100 / 800-628-2783
Fax: 703-683-1523
www.astd.org

The Council of Hotel and Restaurant
    Trainers (CHART)
P.O. Box 2835
Westfield, NJ 07091
Phone: 800-463-5918 / 800-427-5436
www.chart.org

The National Restaurant Association (NRA)
1200 17th Street, NW
Washington, DC 20036
Phone: 202-331-5900
www.restaurant.org

The Institute of Food Technologists (IFT)
221 N. LaSalle Street, Suite 300
Chicago, IL 60601-1291
Phone: 312-782-8424
Fax: 312-782-8348
www.ift.org

HSA International
1601 North Palm Avenue, Suite 211
Pembroke Pines, FL 33026-3241
Phone: 954-432-7301 / 800-432-7302
Fax: 954-432-8677
www.hsainternational.com

The Educational Institute of the American
   Hotel and Motel Association
P.O. Box 531126
Orlando, FL 32853-1126
Phone: 407-999-8100 / 800-752-4567
Fax: 407-236-7848
www.ei-ahma.org

National Executive Housekeepers
   Association, Inc.
1001 Eastwind Drive, Suite 301
Westerville, OH 43081
Phone: 614-895-7166 / 800-200-6342
Fax: 614-895-1248
www.ieha.org

International Council on Hotel, Restaurant,
   and Institutional Education
3205 Skipwith Road
Richmond, VA 23294
Phone: 804-747-4971
Fax: 804-747-5022
www.chrie.org

Appendix B

Additional Resources

For additional information on the topics discussed in this book, refer to the following reading lists, which are organized by subject.

BUSINESS WRITING

American Business English. Karen Bartell. University of Michigan (Ann Arbor), 1995.

Basics of Business Writing (Worksmart Series). Marty Stuckey. Amacom (New York), 1992.

Better Letters: A Handbook of Business and Personal Correspondence. Jan Venolia. Ten Speed Press (Berkeley), 1995.

Effective Business Writing: A Guide for Those Who Write on the Job. Maryann V. Piotrwoski. HarperCollins (New York), 1996.

Improve Your Writing for Work. Elizabeth Chesla. Learning Express (New York), 1997.

The 100 Most Difficult Business Letters You'll Ever Have to Write, Fax, or E-Mail. Bernard Heller. HarperBusiness (New York), 1994.

COLLEGES

Chronicle Vocational School Manual: A Directory of Accredited Vocational and Technical Schools 2000-2001. Chronicle Guidance (Moravia, NY), 2000.

Peterson's Guide to Distance Learning Programs. Peterson's (Lawrenceville, NJ), annual.

Peterson's Guide to Two-Year Colleges. Peterson's (Lawrenceville, NJ), annual.

The College Handbook. College Entrance Examination Board (New York), annual.

COVER LETTERS

Cover Letters Made Easy. Patty Marler and Jan Bailey Mattia. NTC Publishing Group (Lincolnwood, IL), 1995.

Cover Letter Magic. Wendy Enelow and Louise Kursmark. Jist Works (Indianapolis), 2000.

Cover Letters That Knock 'Em Dead. Martin Yates. Adams Media Corp. (Holbrook, MA), 2000.

The Perfect Cover Letter. 2nd Edition. Richard H. Beatty. John Wiley & Sons (New York), 1997.

The Wall Street Journal National Business Employment Weekly: Cover Letters. 3rd Edition. Taunee Besson. John Wiley & Sons (New York), 1999.

FINANCIAL AID

College Costs & Financial Aid Handbook 1999. 19th Edition. College Board. College Entrance Examination Board (New York), 1998.

Financing Your College Degree: A Guide for Adult Students. David F. Finney. College Entrance Examination Board (New York), 1997.

Last Minute College Financing. Daniel Cassidy. Career Press (Franklin Lakes, NJ), 2000.

HOSPITALITY CAREER RESOURCES

Best Impressions in Hospitality. Angie Michaels. Delmar (Albany, NY), 1999.

Career Opportunities in the Food and Beverage Industry. 2nd Edition. Barbara Sims-Bell. Checkmark Books (New York), 2001.

Careers in the Food Services Industry. Robert K. Otterbourg. Barrons Educational Series (New York), 1999.

Choosing a Career in Hotels, Motels, and Resorts. Nancy N. Rue. Rosen Publishing (New York), 1999.

Culinary Math. Linda Block, et al. John Wiley & Sons (New York), 2001.

How To Manage a Successful Bar. Christopher Egerton-Thomas. John Wiley & Sons (New York), 1994.

Managing Hotels Effectively: Lessons from Outstanding General Managers. Eddystone Nebel. John Wiley & Sons (New York), 1991.

Managing the Guest Experience in Hospitality. Robert Ford and Cherill Heaton. Delmar (Albany, NY), 1999.

Principles of Hotel Front Office Operations. Sue Baker, et al. Continuum Books (New York), 2000.

Quality Service: What Every Hospitality Manager Needs to Know. William B. Martin. Prentice Hall (Upper Saddle River, NJ), 2002.

Remarkable Service: A Guide to Winning and Keeping Customers for Servers, Managers, and Restaurant Owners. Culinary Institute of America. John Wiley & Sons (New York), 2001.

Serve 'Em Right: The Complete Guide to Hospitality Service. Ed Solomon, et al. Oak Hill Press (Winchester, VA), 1997.

Service That Sells! The Art of Profitable Hospitality. Phil Roberts. Pencom International (Denver), 1991.

The Complete Restaurant Management Guide. Robert T. Gordon. M.E. Sharpe (Armonk, NY), 1999.

INTERNSHIPS

America's Top Internships. Samer Hamadeh and Mark Oldham. The Princeton Review (New York), annual.

The Yale Daily News Guide to Internships John Anselmi, et al. Kaplan (New York), annual.

INTERVIEWS

101 Great Answers to the Toughest Interview Questions. Ron Fry. Career Press (Franklin Lakes, NJ), 2000.

Great Interview: Successful Strategies for Getting Hired. Vivian Eyre, et al. Learning Express (New York), 2000.

How to Have A Winning Interview. Deborah Bloch. VGM Career Horizons (Lincolnwood, IL), 1998.

Sweaty Palms: The Neglected Art of Being Interviewed. Anthony H. Medley. Ten Speed Press (Berkeley), 1992.

JOB HUNTING

National Job Hotline Directory: The Job Finder's Hot List. Sue Cubbage and Marcia Williams. Planning/Communications (River Forest, IL), 1998.

Occupational Outlook Handbook. U.S. Department of Labor. NTC Publishing Group (Lincolnwood, IL), annual.

What Color Is Your Parachute? 2001: A Practical Manual for Job-Hunters and Career-Changers. Richard Nelson Bolles. Ten Speed Press (Berkeley), 2000.

OFFICE POLITICS

Winning With Difficult People. Arthur Bell and Dayle M. Smith. Barron's Business Success Series (New York), 1997.

Working Relationships: The Simple Truth About Getting Along With Friends and Foes at Work. Bob Wall. Davies-Black (Palo Alto), 1999.

PERIODICALS

Restaurant Industry

Bread & Butter Newsletter (for managers)
National Restaurant Association
1200 17th Street NW
Washington, DC 20036
www.restaurant.org/business/bb/index.cfm

Fork in the Road (for students)
National Restaurant Association
1200 17th Street NW
Washington, DC 20036
www.restaurant.org/careers/fork/index.cfm

Nation's Restaurant News
425 Park Avenue
New York, NY 10022
www.nrn.com

Restaurant Business
P.O. Box 1252
Skokie, IL 60076-9719
www.restaurantbiz.com/restaurantbusiness/
    index.jsp

Restaurant Hospitality
1300 E. 9th Street
Cleveland, OH 44114
http://subscribe.penton.com/rh

Restaurants and Institutions
1350 East Touhy Avenue
P.O. Box 5080
Des Plaines, IL 60017-5080
www.rimag.com

Restaurants USA
National Restaurant Association
1200 17th Street NW
Washington, DC 20036
www.restaurant.org/rusa

Hotel Industry

Hotel & Motel Management
131 West First Street
Duluth, MN 55802
www.hotelmotel.com

Hotels Magazine
1350 East Touhy Avenue
Des Plaines, IL 60018
www.hotelsmag.com

Lodging Magazine
1707 L Street NW, Suite 200
Washington, DC 20036
www.lodgingnews.com

Hospitality

CHRIE *Communique* (newsletter)
International Council On Hotel, Restaurant
    & Institutional Education
3205 Skipwith Road
Richmond, VA 23294-4442

Cornell Hotel and Restaurant Administration
    Quarterly (HRAQ)
School of Hotel Administration
Statler Hall
Cornell University
Ithaca, NY 14853
www.hotelschool.cornell.edu/
    publications/hraq
607-255-3025

Hosteur (Webzine For Future Hospitality &
    Tourism Professionals)
www.chrie.org/public/publications/-
    hosteur/hosteur.html

Hospitality Review
Florida International University
School of Hospitality
North Miami, FL 33181
www.fiu.edu/~review

NEWH Magazine
Network of Executive Women in Hospitality,
    Inc.
P.O. Box 322
Shawano, WI 54166
www.newh.org

RESUMES

Great Resume: Get Noticed, Get Hired. Jason R. Rich. Learning Express (New
    York), 2000.

Resume Magic: Trade Secrets of a Professional Resume Writer. Susan Whitcomb.
    Jist Works (Indianapolis), 1998.

Resumes That Knock 'Em Dead. Martin Yates. Adams Media Corp.
    (Holbrook, MA), 2000.

SCHOLARSHIP GUIDES

Cash for College: The Ultimate Guide to College Scholarships. Cynthia Ruiz McKee and Philip McKee. Quill (New York), 1999.

Complete Office Handbook: The Definitive Resource for Today's Electronic Office. Susan Fenner, et al. Random House (New York), 1996.

How to Go to College Almost for Free: The Secrets of Winning Scholarship Money. Benjamin Kaplan. Harper Resource (New York), 2001.

The Scholarship Book: The Complete Guide to Private-Sector Scholarships, Fellowships, Grants, and Loans for the Undergraduate. Daniel J. Cassidy. Prentice Hall (Upper Saddle River, NJ), annual.

Winning Scholarships for College: An Insider's Guide. Marianne Ragins. Holt (New York), 1999.

STUDYING

How to Study (Basics Made Easy series) 2nd Edition. Gail Wood. Learning Express (New York), 2000.

Read Better, Remember More (Basics Made Easy series) 2nd Edition. Elizabeth Chesla and Jim Gish, Learning Express (New York), 2000.

TEST HELP

Barron's How to Prepare for the SAT: American College Testing Assessment. 12th Edition. George Ehrenhaft, et al. Barron's Educational (New York), 2001.

Cracking the SAT & PSAT. Adam Robinson, et al. Princeton Review (New York), annual.

Appendix C

Directory of Accredited Schools, National Accrediting Associations, and Financial Aid by State

DIRECTORY OF ACCREDITED SCHOOLS BY ACPHA™

The Accreditation Commission for Programs in Hospitality Administration™ (ACPHA™) was established in 1989. To date, the hospitality programs at the following institutions have been granted accreditation by ACPHA™:

Bethune-Cookman College (Daytona Beach, FL)
Buffalo State College (Buffalo, NY)
California State Polytechnic University, Pomona (Pomona, CA)
Delaware State University (Dover, DE)
Drexel University (Philadelphia, PA)
Georgia State University (Atlanta, GA)
Indiana University of Pennsylvania (Indiana, PA)
Iowa State University (Ames, IA)
James Madison University (Harrisonburg, VA)
Johnson and Wales University (Providence, RI)
Kansas State University (Manhattan, KS)
Mercyhurst College (Erie, PA)
New York City Technical College (New York, NY)
Niagara University (Niagara Falls, NY)
Northeastern State University (Tahlequah, OK)
Northern Arizona University (Flagstaff, AZ)

Oklahoma State University (Stillwater, OK)
Purdue University (West Lafayette, IN)
Rochester Institute of Technology (Rochester, NY)
Southern Illinois University (Carbondale, IL)
Southwest Missouri State University (Springfield, MO)
Texas Tech University (Lubbock, TX)
University of Central Florida (Orlando, FL)
University of Hawaii (Manoa, HI)
University of Massachusetts (Amherst, MA)
University of Missouri (Columbia, MO)
University of New Hampshire (Durham, NH)
University of New Orleans (New Orleans, LA)
University of North Texas (Denton, TX)
University of South Carolina (Columbia, SC)
Virginia Polytechnic Institute & State University (Blacksburg, VA)
Virginia State University (Petersburg, VA)
Widener University (Chester, PA)

Contact:
Accreditation Commission for Programs in Hospitality Administration™
    (ACPHA™)
Diana Newmier, Chairperson
Sodexho
Corporate Vice President, Human Resources
9801 Washingtonian Boulevard, Suite 1136
Gaithersburg, MD 20878
Phone: 301-987-4185
Fax: 301-987-4186

DIRECTORY OF ACCREDITED SCHOOLS BY CAHM

The Commission for Accreditation of Hospitality Management Programs (CAHM) accredits hospitality management programs at the associate-degree or equivalent level. At press time, these institutions had received CAHM accreditation:

American Institute of Commerce (Davenport, IA)
Columbus State Community College (Columbus, OH)
Community College of Southern Nevada (Cheyenne, NV)
Domino Carlton Tivoli-International Hotel & Management Institute (Lucerne, FL)
Erie Community College, North Campus (Williamsville, NY)
Florida Community College (Jacksonville, FL)
Horry Georgetown Technical College (Conway, SC)
Ivy Tech State College (East Chicago, IN)
Kapi'olani Community College (Honolulu, HI)
Metropolitan Community College (Omaha, NE)
Northwestern Business College (Chicago, IL)
Parkland College (Champaign, IL)
Pennsylvania College of Technology (Williamsport, PA)
Sinclair Community College (Dayton, OH)
Trident Technical College (Charleston, SC)
Utah Valley State College (Orem, UT)

Contact:
Commission for Accreditation of Hospitality Management Programs (CAHM)
Josette Katz, Ph.D., Chair
Atlantic Community College
Business/Hospitality Management
5100 Blackhorse Pike
Mays Landing, NJ 08330
Phone: 609-343-5094
Fax: 609-343-5122

NATIONAL ACCREDITING AGENCIES

Here is a list of national accrediting agencies for you to contact to see if your chosen school is accredited. You can request a list of schools that each agency accredits.

Accrediting Commission for Career Schools
    and Colleges of Technology (ACCSCT)
2101 Wilson Boulevard, Suite 302
Arlington, VA 22201
Phone: 703-247-4212
Fax: 703-247-4533
www.accsct.org

Accrediting Council for Independent
    Colleges and Schools (ACICS)
750 First Street NE, Suite 980
Washington, DC 20002-4241
Phone: 202-336-6780
Fax: 202-842-2593
www.acics.org

Distance Education and Training Council
    (DETC)
1601 Eighteenth Street NW
Washington, DC 20009-2529
Phone: 202-234-5100
Fax: 202-332-1386
www.detc.org

REGIONAL ACCREDITING AGENCIES

Middle States
Middle States Association of Colleges and
    Schools
Commission on Institutions of Higher
    Education
3624 Market Street
Philadelphia, PA 19104-2680
Phone: 215-662-5606
Fax: 215-662-5950
www.msache.org

New England States
New England Association of Schools and
    Colleges
Commission on Institutions of Higher
    Education (NEASC-CIHE)
209 Burlington Road
Bedford, MA 07130-1433
Phone: 781-271-0022, x313
Fax: 781-271-0950
www.neasc.org/cihe

New England Association of Schools and
   Colleges
Commission on Vocational, Technical and
   Career Institution (NEASC-CTCI)
209 Burlington Road
Bedford, MA 01730-1433
Phone: 781-271-0022, x316
Fax: 781-271-0950
www.neasc.org/ctci

North Central States

North Central Association of Colleges and
   Schools
Commission on Institutions of Higher
   Education (NCA)
30 North LaSalle, Suite 2400
Chicago, IL 60602-2504
Phone: 312-263-0456 / 800-621-7440
Fax: 312-263-7462
www.ncahihe.org

Northwest States

Northwest Association of Schools and
   Colleges
Commission on Colleges
11130 NE 33rd Place, Suite 120
Bellevue, WA 98004
Phone: 425-827-2005
Fax: 425-827-3395
www.cocnase.org

Southern States

Southern Association of Colleges and
   Schools
Commission on Colleges (SACS)
1866 Southern Lane
Decatur, GA 30033-4097
Phone: 404-679-4500 / 800-248-7701
Fax: 404-679-4558
www.sacscoc.org

Western States

Western Association of Schools and
   Colleges
Accrediting Commission for Community and
   Junior Colleges (WASC-Jr.)
3402 Mendocino Avenue
Santa Rosa, CA 95403-2244
Phone: 707-569-9177
Fax: 707-569-9179
www.accjc.org

Western Association of Schools and
   Colleges
Accrediting Commission for Senior Colleges
   and Universities (WASC-Sr.)
985 Atlantic Avenue, Suite 100
Alameda, CA 94501
Phone: 510-632-5000
Fax: 510-632-8361
www.wascsenior.org/senior/wascsr.html

FINANCIAL AID FROM STATE HIGHER EDUCATION AGENCIES

You can request information about financial aid from each of the following state higher education agencies and governing boards.

ALABAMA

Alabama Commission on Higher Education
100 North Union Street
P.O. Box 302000
Montgomery 36130-2000
334-281-1998; fax 334-242-0268
www.ache.state.al.us

State Department of Education
50 North Ripley Street
P.O. Box 302101
Montgomery 36104
205-242-8082
www.alsde.edu

ALASKA

Alaska Commission on Postsecondary
    Education
3030 Vintage Boulevard
Juneau 99801-7100
907-465-2962; 800-441-2962;
    fax 907-465-5316
www.state.ak.us/acpe

State Department of Education
801 W. 10th Street, Suite 200
Juneau 99801
907-465-2800; fax 907-465-3452
www.educ.state.ak.us

ARIZONA

Arizona Board of Regents
2020 N. Central Avenue, Suite 230
Phoenix 85004-4593
602-229-2500; fax 602-229-2555
www.abor.asu.edu

State Department of Education
1535 West Jefferson Street
Phoenix 85007
602-542-4361; 800-352-4558
www.ade.state.az.us

ARKANSAS

Arkansas Department of Higher Education
144 E. Capitol Avenue
Little Rock 72201
501-371-2000
www.arkansashighered.com

Arkansas Department of Education
4 State Capitol Mall, Room 304A
Little Rock 72201-1071
501-682-4474
arkedu.state.ar.us

CALIFORNIA

California Student Aid Commission
P.O. Box 419027
Rancho Cordova 95741-9027
916-445-0880; 888-224-7268;
    fax 916-526-8002
www.csac.ca.gov

California Department of Education
721 Capitol Mall
Sacramento 95814
916-657-2451
http://goldmine.cde.ca.gov

COLORADO

Colorado Commission on Higher Education
1380 Lawrence Street, Suite 1200
Denver 80204
303-866-2723; fax 303-866-4266
www.state.co.us/cche_dir/hecche.html

State Department of Education
201 East Colfax Avenue
Denver 80203-1799
303-866-6600; fax 303-830-0793
www.cde.state.co.us

CONNECTICUT

Connecticut Department of Higher Education
61 Woodland Street
Hartford 06105-2326
860-947-1800; fax 860-947-1310
www.ctdhe.org

Connecticut Department of Education
P.O. Box 2219
Hartford 06145
860-566-5677
www.state.ct.us/sde

DELAWARE

Delaware Higher Education Commission
820 N. French Street
Wilmington 19801
302-577-3240; 800-292-7935;
    fax 302-577-5765
www.doe.state.de.us/high-ed

DISTRICT OF COLUMBIA

Department of Human Services
Office of Postsecondary Education,
    Research, and Assistance
2100 Martin Luther King Jr. Avenue SE,
    Suite 401
Washington 20020
202-727-3685

District of Columbia Public Schools
Division of Student Services
4501 Lee Street NE
Washington 20019
202-724-4934
www.k12.dc.us

FLORIDA

Florida Department of Education
Turlington Building
325 West Gaines Street
Tallahassee 32399-0400
904-487-0649
www.firn.edu/doe

GEORGIA

Georgia Student Finance Commission

State Loans and Grants Division

Suite 245, 2082 E. Exchange Place

Tucker 30084

404-414-3000

www.gsfc.org

State Department of Education

2054 Twin Towers E., 205 Butler Street

Atlanta 30334-5040

404-656-5812

www.glc.k12.state.ga.us

HAWAII

Hawaii Department of Education

2530 10th Avenue, Room A12

Honolulu 96816

808-733-9103

www.doe.k12.hi.us

IDAHO

Idaho Board of Education

P.O. Box 83720

Boise 83720-0037

208-334-2270

www.sde.state.id.us/osbe/board.htm

State Department of Education

650 West State Street

Boise 83720

208-332-6800

www.sde.state.id.us

ILLINOIS

Illinois Student Assistance Commission

1755 Lake Cook Road

Deerfield 60015-5209

708-948-8500

www.isac1.org

INDIANA

State Student Assistance Commission of
Indiana

150 W. Market Street, Suite 500

Indianapolis 46204-2811

317-232-2350; 888-528-4719;
fax 317-232-3260

www.in.gov/ssaci

Indiana Department of Education

Room 229, State House

Indianapolis 46204-2798

317-232-2305

ideanet.doe.state.in.us

IOWA

Iowa College Student Aid Commission

200 10th Street, 4th Floor

Des Moines 50309-2036

515-242-3344

www.state.ia.us/collegeaid

Iowa Department of Education

Grimes State Office Building

Des Moines 50319-0146

515-281-5294; fax 515-242-5988

www.state.ia.us/educate

KANSAS

Kansas Board of Regents

1000 SW Jackson Street, Suite 520

Topeka 66612-1368

785-296-3421

www.kansasregents.org

State Department of Education

Kansas State Education Building

120 E. Tenth Avenue

Topeka 66612-1103

785-296-3201; fax 785-296-7933

www.ksbe.state.ks.us

KENTUCKY

Kentucky Higher Education Assistance

   Authority

Suite 102, 1050 U.S. 127 South

Frankfort 40601-4323

800-928-8926

www.kheaa.com

State Department of Education

500 Mero Street

Frankfort 40601

502-564-4770; 800-533-5372

www.kde.state.ky.us

LOUISIANA

Louisiana Student Financial Assistance

   Commission

Office of Student Financial Assistance

P.O. Box 91202

Baton Rouge 70821-9202

800-259-5626

www.osfa.state.la.us

State Department of Education

P.O. Box 94064

626 North 4th Street, 12th Floor

Baton Rouge 70804-9064

504-342-2098; 877-453-2721

www.doe.state.la.us

MAINE

Finance Authority of Maine

5 Community Drive

P.O. Box 949

Augusta 04333-0949

207-287-3263; 800-228-3734;

   fax 207-623-0095

www.famemaine.com/html/education

Maine Department of Education

23 State House Station

Augusta 04333-0023

207-287-5800; fax 207-287-5900

www.state.me.us/education

MARYLAND

Maryland Higher Education Commission

Jeffrey Building, 16 Francis Street

Annapolis 21401-1781

410-974-2971

www.mhec.state.md.us

Maryland State Department of Education

200 West Baltimore Street

Baltimore 21201-2595

410-767-0100

www.msde.state.md.us

MASSACHUSETTS

Massachusetts Board of Higher Education

One Ashburton Place, Room 1401

Boston 02108

617-727-9420

www.mass.edu

State Department of Education

350 Main Street

Malden 02148-5023

781-338-3300

www.doe.mass.edu

Massachusetts Higher Education Information
Center

700 Boylston Street

Boston 02116

617-536-0200; 877-332-4348

www.heic.org

MICHIGAN

Michigan Higher Education Assistance
Authority

Office of Scholarships and Grants

P.O. Box 30462

Lansing 48909-7962

517-373-3394; 877-323-2287

www.mi-studentaid.org

Michigan Department of Education

608 W. Allegan Street, Hannah Building

Lansing 48909

517-373-3324

www.mde.state.mi.us

MINNESOTA

Minnesota Higher Education Services Office

1450 Energy Park Drive, Suite 350

Saint Paul 55108-5227

651-642-0533; 800-657-3866;
 fax: 651-642-0675

www.mheso.state.mn.us

Department of Children, Families, and
Learning

1500 Highway 36 West

Roseville, MN 55113

651-582-8200

www.educ.state.mn.us

MISSISSIPPI

Mississippi Postsecondary Education
Financial Assistance Board

3825 Ridgewood Road

Jackson 39211-6453

601-982-6663

www.ihl.state.ms.us

State Department of Education

Central High School, P.O. Box 771

359 North West Street

Jackson 39205-0771

601-359-3513

www.mde.k12.ms.us

MISSOURI

Missouri Coordinating Board for Higher
Education

3515 Amazonas Drive

Jefferson City 65109-5717

314-751-2361; 800-473-6757;
 fax 573-751-6635

www.cbhe.state.mo.us

Missouri State Department of Elementary
and Secondary Education
P.O. Box 480
Jefferson City 65102-0480
573-751-4212; fax 573-751-8613
www.dese.state.mo.us

MONTANA

Montana Higher Education Student
Assistance Corporation
2500 Broadway
Helena 59620-3104
406-444-6597; 1-800-852-2761 x 0606;
fax 406-444-0684
www.mhesac.org

Montana Office of the Commissioner of
Higher Education
2500 Broadway
P.O. Box 203101
Helena 59620-3101
406-444-6570; fax 406-444-1469
www.montana.edu/wwwoche

State Office of Public Instruction
P.O. Box 202501
Helena 59620-2501
406-444-3680; 888-231-9393
www.metnet.state.mt.us

NEBRASKA

Coordinating Commission for Postsecondary
Education
P.O. Box 95005
Lincoln 68509-5005
402-471-2847; fax 402-471-2886
www.ccpe.state.ne.us

Nebraska Department of Education
301 Centennial Mall South
Lincoln 68509-4987
402-471-2295
www.nde.state.ne.us

NEVADA

Nevada Department of Education
700 East Fifth Street
Carson City 89701-5096
775-687-9200; fax 775-687-9101
www.nde.state.nv.us

NEW HAMPSHIRE

New Hampshire Postsecondary Education
Commission
2 Industrial Park Drive
Concord 03301-8512
603-271-2555; fax 603-271-2696
www.state.nh.us/postsecondary

State Department of Education
State Office Park South
101 Pleasant Street
Concord 03301
603-271-3494; fax 603-271-1953
www.state.nh.us/doe

NEW JERSEY

State of New Jersey
20 West State Street
P.O. Box 542
Trenton 08625-0542
609-292-4310; fax 609-292-7225;
800-792-8670
www.state.nj.us/highereducation

State Department of Education
225 West State Street
Trenton 08625-0500
609-984-6409
www.state.nj.us/education

NEW MEXICO

New Mexico Commission on Higher
    Education
1068 Cerrillos Road
Santa Fe 87501-4925
505-827-7383; fax 505-827-7392
www.nmche.org

State Department of Education
Education Building
300 Don Gaspar
Santa Fe 87501-2786
505-827-6648
www.sde.state.nm.us

NEW YORK

New York State Higher Education Services
    Corporation
One Commerce Plaza
Albany 12255
518-473-1574; 888-697-4372
www.hesc.state.ny.us

State Education Department
89 Washington Avenue
Albany 12234
518-474-3852
www.nysed.gov

NORTH CAROLINA

North Carolina State Education Assistance
    Authority
P.O. Box 14103
Research Triangle Park 27709
919-549-8614; fax 919-549-8481
www.ncseaa.edu

State Department of Public Instruction
301 North Wilmington Street
Raleigh 27601
919-807-3300
www.dpi.state.nc.us

NORTH DAKOTA

North Dakota University System/
    State Board of Higher Education
10th Floor, State Capitol
600 East Boulevard Avenue,
    Department 215
Bismarck 58505-0230
701-328-2960; fax 701-328-2961
www.ndus.edu/sbhe

State Department of Public Instruction
State Capitol Building, 11th Floor
600 E. Boulevard Avenue, Department 201
Bismarck 58505-0164
701-328-2260; fax 701-328-2461
www.dpi.state.nd.us

OHIO

State Department of Education
25 South Front Street
Columbus 43266-0308
614-466-2761; 877-644-6338
www.ode.state.oh.us

OKLAHOMA

Oklahoma State Regents for Higher
   Education
655 Research Parkway, Suite 200
Oklahoma City 73104
405-225-9100; fax 405-225-9230
www.okhighered.org

Oklahoma Guaranteed Student Loan
   Program
P.O. Box 3000
Oklahoma City 73101-3000
405-858-4300; fax 405-234-4390;
   800-247-0420
www.ogslp.org

State Department of Education
Oliver Hodge Memorial Education Building
2500 North Lincoln Boulevard
Oklahoma City 73105-4599
405-521-4122; fax 405-521-6205
www.sde.state.ok.us

OREGON

Oregon Student Assistance Commission
1500 Valley River Drive, Suite 100
Eugene 97401-2130
503-687-7400
www.osac.state.or.us

Oregon State System of Higher Education
P.O. Box 3175
Eugene 97403
541-346-5700
www.ous.edu

Oregon Department of Education
255 Capitol Street NE
Salem 97310-0203
503-378-3569; fax 503-378-2892
www.ode.state.or.us

PENNSYLVANIA

Pennsylvania Higher Education Assistance
   Agency
1200 North Seventh Street
Harrisburg 17102-1444
800-692-7392
www.pheaa.org

RHODE ISLAND

Rhode Island Office of Higher Education
301 Promenade Street
Providence 02908-5748
401-222-2088; fax 401-222-2545
www.ribghe.org

Rhode Island Higher Education Assistance
   Authority
560 Jefferson Boulevard
Warwick 02886
800-922-9855; fax 401-736-1100
www.riheaa.org

State Department of Education
225 Westminster Street
Providence 02903
401-222-4600
www.ridoe.net

SOUTH CAROLINA

South Carolina Higher Education Tuition
  Grants Commission
101 Business Park Boulevard, Suite 2100
Columbia 29203-9498
803-896-1120; fax 803-896-1126
www.sctuitiongrants.com

State Department of Education
1429 Senate Street
Columbia 29201
803-734-8500
www.sde.state.sc.us

SOUTH DAKOTA

Department of Education and Cultural Affairs
700 Governors Drive
Pierre 57501-2291
605-773-3134
www.state.sd.us/deca

South Dakota Board of Regents
306 East Capitol Avenue, Suite 200
Pierre 57501-2409
605-773-3455
www.ris.sdbor.edu

TENNESSEE

Tennessee Higher Education Commission
404 James Robertson Parkway, Suite 1900
Nashville 37243-0820
615-741-3605; fax 615-741-6230
www.state.tn.us/thec

State Department of Education
Andrew Johnson Tower, 6th Floor
710 James Robertson Parkway
Nashville 37243-0375
615-741-2731
www.state.tn.us/education

TEXAS

Texas Education Agency
1701 North Congress Avenue
Austin 78701-1494
512-463-9734
www.tea.state.tx.us

Texas Higher Education Coordinating Board
P.O. Box 12788
Austin 78711
512-427-6101; 800-242-3062
www.thecb.state.tx.us

UTAH

Utah System of Higher Education
#3 Triad Center, Suite 550
Salt Lake City 84180-1205
801-321-7101
www.utahsbr.edu

Utah State Office of Education
250 East 500 South
Salt Lake City 84111
801-538-7500; fax 801-538-7521
www.usoe.k12.ut.us

VERMONT

Vermont Student Assistance Corporation

Champlain Mill

P.O. Box 2000

Winooski 05404-2601

802-655-9602; 800-642-3177;

   fax 802-654-3765

www.vsac.org

Vermont Department of Education

120 State Street

Montpelier 05620-2501

802-828-3147; fax 802-828-3140

www.state.vt.us/educ

VIRGINIA

State Council of Higher Education for

   Virginia

James Monroe Building

101 North 14th Street

Richmond 23219

804-225-2628; fax 804-225-2638

www.schev.edu

State Department of Education

P.O. Box 2120

Richmond 23218-2120

800-292-3820

www.pen.k12.va.us

WASHINGTON

Washington State Higher Education

   Coordinating Board

P.O. Box 43430

917 Lakeridge Way, SW

Olympia 98504-3430

206-753-7800

www.hecb.wa.gov

State Department of Public Instruction

Old Capitol Building

P.O. Box 47200

Olympia 98504-7200

360-725-6000

www.k12.wa.us

WEST VIRGINIA

State Department of Education

1900 Kanawha Boulevard East

Charleston 25305

304-558-2691

wvde.state.wv.us

State College and University Systems of

   West Virginia Central Office

1018 Kanawha Boulevard East, Suite 700

Charleston 25301-2827

304-558-2101; fax 304-558-5719

www.hepc.wvnet.edu

WISCONSIN

Higher Educational Aids Board

P.O. Box 7885

Madison 53707-7885

608-267-2206; fax 608-267-2808

www.heab.state.wi.us

State Department of Public Instruction

125 South Webster Street

P.O. Box 7841

Madison 53707-7814

608-266-3390; 800-541-4563

www.dpi.state.wi.us

WYOMING

Wyoming State Department of Education

Hathaway Building

2300 Capitol Avenue, 2nd Floor

Cheyenne 82002-0050

307-777-7675; fax 307-777-6234

www.k12.wy.us/wdehome.html

Wyoming Community College Commission

2020 Carey Avenue, 8th Floor

Cheyenne 82002

307-777-7763; fax 307-777-6567

www.commission.wcc.edu

PUERTO RICO

Council on Higher Education

P.O. Box 19900

San Juan 00910-1900

787-724-7100

www.ces.gobierno.pr

Department of Education

P. O. Box 190759

San Juan 00919-0759

809-759-2000; fax 809-250-0275

www.de.prstar.net

U.S. DEPARTMENT OF EDUCATION

Students.Gov (Students' Gateway to the
U.S. Government)

400 Maryland Avenue SW

ROB-3, Room 4004

Washington, DC 20202-5132

www.students.gov

U.S. Department of Education

Office of Postsecondary Education

1990 K Street NW

Washington, DC 20006

www.ed.gov/offices/OPE

Appendix D

Sample Free Application for Federal Student Aid (FAFSA)

On the following pages you will find a sample FAFSA. Use this sample to familiarize yourself with the form so that when you apply for federal, and state student grants, work-study, and loans, you will know what information you need to have ready. At print this was the most current form, and although the form remains mostly the same from year to year, you should check the FAFSA website (www.fafsa.ed.gov) for the most current information.

2001-2002

The FAFSA

July 1, 2001 — June 30, 2002
Free Application for Federal Student Aid

OMB # 1845-0001

Use this form to apply for federal and state* student grants, work-study, and loans.

Apply over the Internet with  **www.fafsa.ed.gov**

 If you are filing a **2000 income tax return,** we recommend that you complete it before filling out this form. However, you do not need to file your income tax return with the IRS before you submit this form.

If you or your family has **unusual circumstances** (such as loss of employment) that might affect your need for student financial aid, submit this form, and then consult with the financial aid office at the college you plan to attend.

You may also use this form to apply for **aid from other sources, such as your state or college.** The deadlines for states (see table to right) or colleges may be as early as January 2001 and may differ. You may be required to complete additional forms. Check with your high school guidance counselor or a financial aid administrator at your college about state and college sources of student aid.

 Your answers on this form will be read electronically. Therefore:

- use black ink and fill in ovals completely:

  Yes ● **No** ✕ ✓

- print clearly in CAPITAL letters and skip a box between words:

  | 1 | 5 | | E | L | M | | S | T |

- report dollar amounts (such as $12,356.41) like this:

  $ | | 1 | 2 | , | 3 | 5 | 6 | **no cents**

Green is for students and purple is for parents.

If you have questions about this application, or for more information on eligibility requirements and the U.S. Department of Education's student aid programs, look on the Internet at **www.ed.gov/studentaid** You can also call 1-800-4FED-AID (1-800-433-3243) seven days a week from 8:00 a.m. through midnight (Eastern time). TTY users may call 1-800-730-8913.

 After you complete this application, make a copy of it for your records. Then **send the original of pages 3 through 6** in the attached envelope or send it to: Federal Student Aid Programs, P.O. Box 4008, Mt. Vernon, IL 62864-8608.

You should submit your application as early as possible, but no earlier than January 1, 2001. We must receive your application **no later than July 1, 2002.** Your school must have your correct, complete information by your last day of enrollment in the 2001-2002 school year.

You should hear from us within four weeks. If you do not, please call 1-800-433-3243 or check on-line at www.fafsa.ed.gov

 Now go to page 3 and begin filling out this form.
Refer to the notes as needed.

STATE AID DEADLINES

AR	April 1, 2001 *(date received)*
AZ	June 30, 2002 *(date received)*
*^ CA	March 2, 2001 *(date postmarked)*
* DC	June 24, 2001 *(date received by state)*
DE	April 15, 2001 *(date received)*
FL	May 15, 2001 *(date processed)*
HI	March 1, 2001
^ IA	July 1, 2001 *(date received)*
IL	First-time applicants – September 30, 2001 Continuing applicants – July 15, 2001 *(date received)*
^ IN	For priority consideration – March 1, 2001 *(date postmarked)*
* KS	For priority consideration – April 1, 2001 *(date received)*
KY	For priority consideration – March 15, 2001 *(date received)*
^ LA	For priority consideration – April 15, 2001 Final deadline – July 1, 2001 *(date received)*
^ MA	For priority consideration – May 1, 2001 *(date received)*
MD	March 1, 2001 *(date postmarked)*
ME	May 1, 2001 *(date received)*
MI	High school seniors – February 21, 2001 College students – March 21, 2001 *(date received)*
MN	June 30, 2002 *(date received)*
MO	April 1, 2001 *(date received)*
MT	For priority consideration – March 1, 2001 *(date postmarked)*
NC	March 15, 2001 *(date received)*
ND	April 15, 2001 *(date processed)*
NH	May 1, 2001 *(date received)*
^ NJ	June 1, 2001 if you received a Tuition Aid Grant in 2000-2001 All other applicants – October 1, 2001, for fall and spring terms – March 1, 2002, for spring term only *(date received)*
*^ NY	May 1, 2002 *(date postmarked)*
OH	October 1, 2001 *(date received)*
OK	For priority consideration – April 30, 2001 Final deadline – June 30, 2001 *(date received)*
OR	May 1, 2002 *(date received)*
* PA	All 2000-2001 State Grant recipients and all non-2000-2001 State Grant recipients in degree programs – May 1, 2001 All other applicants – August 1, 2001 *(date received)*
PR	May 2, 2002 *(date application signed)*
RI	March 1, 2001 *(date received)*
SC	June 30, 2001 *(date received)*
TN	May 1, 2001 *(date processed)*
*^ WV	March 1, 2001 *(date received)*

Check with your financial aid administrator for these states: AK, AL, *AS, *CT, CO, *FM, GA, *GU, ID, *MH, *MP, MS, *NE, *NM, *NV, *PW, *SD, *TX, UT, *VA, *VI, *VT, WA, WI, and *WY.

^ *Applicants encouraged to obtain proof of mailing.*
* *Additional form may be required*

STATE AID DEADLINES

Notes for questions 13–14 (page 3)

If you are an eligible noncitizen, write in your eight or nine digit Alien Registration Number. Generally, you are an eligible noncitizen if you are: (1) a U.S. permanent resident and you have an Alien Registration Receipt Card (I-551); (2) a conditional permanent resident (I-551C); or (3) an other eligible noncitizen with an Arrival-Departure Record (I-94) from the U.S. Immigration and Naturalization Service showing any one of the following designations: "Refugee," "Asylum Granted," "Indefinite Parole," "Humanitarian Parole," or "Cuban-Haitian Entrant." If you are in the U.S. on only an F1 or F2 student visa, or only a J1 or J2 exchange visitor visa, or a G series visa (pertaining to international organizations), you must fill in oval c. If you are neither a citizen nor eligible noncitizen, you are not eligible for federal student aid. However, you may be eligible for state or college aid.

Notes for questions 17–21 (page 3)

For undergraduates, full time generally means taking at least 12 credit hours in a term or 24 clock hours per week. 3/4 time generally means taking at least 9 credit hours in a term or 18 clock hours per week. Half time generally means taking at least 6 credit hours in a term or 12 clock hours per week. Provide this information about the college you plan to attend.

Notes for question 29 (page 3) — Enter the correct number in the box in question 29.

Enter 1 for 1st bachelor's degree
Enter 2 for 2nd bachelor's degree
Enter 3 for associate degree (occupational or technical program)
Enter 4 for associate degree (general education or transfer program)
Enter 5 for certificate or diploma for completing an occupational, technical, or educational program of less than two years

Enter 6 for certificate or diploma for completing an occupational, technical, or educational program of at least two years
Enter 7 for teaching credential program (nondegree program)
Enter 8 for graduate or professional degree
Enter 9 for other/undecided

Notes for question 30 (page 3) — Enter the correct number in the box in question 30.

Enter 0 for 1st year undergraduate/never attended college
Enter 1 for 1st year undergraduate/attended college before
Enter 2 for 2nd year undergraduate/sophomore
Enter 3 for 3rd year undergraduate/junior

Enter 4 for 4th year undergraduate/senior
Enter 5 for 5th year/other undergraduate
Enter 6 for 1st year graduate/professional
Enter 7 for continuing graduate/professional or beyond

Notes for questions 37 c. and d. (page 4) and 71 c. and d. (page 5)

If you filed or will file a foreign tax return, or a tax return with Puerto Rico, Guam, American Samoa, the Virgin Islands, the Marshall Islands, the Federated States of Micronesia, or Palau, use the information from that return to fill out this form. If you filed a foreign return, convert all figures to U.S. dollars, using the exchange rate that is in effect today.

Notes for questions 38 (page 4) and 72 (page 5)

In general, a person is eligible to file a 1040A or 1040EZ if he or she makes less than $50,000, does not itemize deductions, does not receive income from his or her own business or farm, and does not receive alimony. A person is not eligible if he or she itemizes deductions, receives self-employment income or alimony, or is required to file Schedule D for capital gains.

Notes for questions 41 (page 4) and 75 (page 5) — only for people who filed a 1040EZ or Telefile

On the 1040EZ, if a person answered "Yes" on line 5, use EZ worksheet line F to determine the number of exemptions ($2,800 equals one exemption). If a person answered "No" on line 5, enter 01 if he or she is single, or 02 if he or she is married.

On the Telefile, use line J to determine the number of exemptions ($2,800 equals one exemption).

Notes for questions 47–48 (page 4) and 81–82 (page 5)

Net worth means current value minus debt. If net worth is one million or more, enter $999,999. If net worth is negative, enter 0.

Investments include real estate (do not include the home you live in), trust funds, money market funds, mutual funds, certificates of deposit, stocks, stock options, bonds, other securities, education IRAs, installment and land sale contracts (including mortgages held), commodities, etc. Investment value includes the market value of these investments as of today. Investment debt means only those debts that are related to the investments.

Investments do not include the home you live in, cash, savings, checking accounts, the value of life insurance and retirement plans (pension funds, annuities, noneducation IRAs, Keogh plans, etc.), or the value of prepaid tuition plans.

Business and/or investment farm value includes the market value of land, buildings, machinery, equipment, inventory, etc. Business and/or investment farm debt means only those debts for which the business or investment farm was used as collateral.

Notes for question 58 (page 4)

Answer **"No"** (you are not a veteran) if you (1) have never engaged in active duty in the U.S. Armed Forces, (2) are currently an ROTC student or a cadet or midshipman at a service academy, or (3) are a National Guard or Reserves enlistee activated only for training. Also answer "No" if you are currently serving in the U.S. Armed Forces and will continue to serve through June 30, 2002.

Answer **"Yes"** (you are a veteran) if you (1) have engaged in active duty in the U.S. Armed Forces (Army, Navy, Air Force, Marines, or Coast Guard) or as a member of the National Guard or Reserves who was called to active duty for purposes other than training, or were a cadet or midshipman at one of the service academies, **and** (2) were released under a condition other than dishonorable. Also answer "Yes" if you are not a veteran now but will be one by June 30, 2002.

the 2001-2002 FAFSA

Free Application for Federal Student Aid
For July 1, 2001 — June 30, 2002

OMB # 1845-0001

Step One: For questions 1-34, leave blank any questions that do not apply to you (the student).

1-3. Your full name (as it appears on your Social Security Card)

1. LAST NAME — FOR INFORMATION ONLY
2. FIRST NAME — DO NOT SUBMIT
3. MIDDLE INITIAL

4-7. Your permanent mailing address

4. NUMBER AND STREET (INCLUDE APT. NUMBER)
5. CITY (AND COUNTRY IF NOT U.S.)
6. STATE
7. ZIP CODE

8. Your Social Security Number — XXX – XX – XXXX

9. Your date of birth — / / 19

10. Your permanent telephone number — ( ) –

11-12. Your driver's license number and state (if any)

11. LICENSE NUMBER
12. STATE

13. Are you a U.S. citizen? Pick one. **See Page 2.**
- **a.** Yes, I am a U.S. citizen. .... ○ 1
- **b.** No, but I am an eligible noncitizen. **Fill in question 14.** ...... ○ 2
- **c.** No, I am not a citizen or eligible noncitizen. .... ○ 3

14. ALIEN REGISTRATION NUMBER — A

15. What is your marital status as of today?
- I am single, divorced, or widowed. ○ 1
- I am married/remarried. ○ 2
- I am separated. ○ 3

16. Month and year you were married, separated, divorced, or widowed — MONTH / YEAR

For each question (17 - 21), please mark whether you will be full time, 3/4 time, half time, less than half time, or not attending. **See page 2.**

		Full time/Not sure	3/4 time	Half time	Less than half time	Not attending
17.	Summer 2001	○ 1	○ 2	○ 3	○ 4	○ 5
18.	Fall 2001	○ 1	○ 2	○ 3	○ 4	○ 5
19.	Winter 2001-2002	○ 1	○ 2	○ 3	○ 4	○ 5
20.	Spring 2002	○ 1	○ 2	○ 3	○ 4	○ 5
21.	Summer 2002	○ 1	○ 2	○ 3	○ 4	○ 5

22. Highest school your father completed — Middle school/Jr. High ○ 1   High school ○ 2   College or beyond ○ 3   Other/unknown ○ 4

23. Highest school your mother completed — Middle school/Jr. High ○ 1   High school ○ 2   College or beyond ○ 3   Other/unknown ○ 4

24. What is your state of legal residence? STATE

25. Did you become a legal resident of this state before January 1, 1996? — Yes ○ 1   No ○ 2

26. If the answer to question 25 is **"No,"** give month and year you became a legal resident. — MONTH / YEAR

27. Are you male? (Most male students must register with Selective Service to get federal aid.) — Yes ○ 1   No ○ 2

28. If you are male (age 18-25) and not registered, do you want Selective Service to register you? — Yes ○ 1   No ○ 2

29. What degree or certificate will you be working on during 2001-2002? **See page 2** and enter the correct number in the box.

30. What will be your grade level when you begin the 2001-2002 school year? **See page 2** and enter the correct number in the box.

31. Will you have a high school diploma or GED before you enroll? — Yes ○ 1   No ○ 2

32. Will you have your first bachelor's degree before July 1, 2001? — Yes ○ 1   No ○ 2

33. In addition to grants, are you interested in student loans (which you must pay back)? — Yes ○ 1   No ○ 2

34. In addition to grants, are you interested in "work-study" (which you earn through work)? — Yes ○ 1   No ○ 2

35. Do not leave this question blank. Have you ever been convicted of possessing or selling illegal drugs? If you have, answer "Yes," complete and submit this application, and we will send you a worksheet in the mail for you to determine if your conviction affects your eligibility for aid. — No ○ 1   Yes ○ 3

DO NOT LEAVE QUESTION 35 BLANK

Step Two:
For questions 36-49, report your (the student's) income and assets. If you are married, report your spouse's income and assets, even if you were not married in 2000. Ignore references to "spouse" if you are currently single, separated, divorced, or widowed.

36. For 2000, have you (the student) completed your IRS income tax return or another tax return listed in **question 37**?

a. I have already completed my return. ○ 1   **b.** I will file, but I have not yet ○ 2   **c.** I'm not going to file. **(Skip to question 42.)** ○ 3
completed my return.

37. What income tax return did you file or will you file for 2000?

a. IRS 1040 .... ○ 1   **d.** A tax return for Puerto Rico, Guam, American Samoa, the Virgin Islands, the
b. IRS 1040A, 1040EZ, 1040Telefile ...... ○ 2   Marshall Islands, the Federated States of Micronesia, or Palau. **See Page 2.** ...... ○ 4
c. A foreign tax return. **See Page 2.** ...... ○ 3

38. If you have filed or will file a 1040, were you eligible to file a 1040A or 1040EZ? **See page 2.**   Yes ○ 1   No ○ 2   Don't ○ 3 Know

For questions 39-51, if the answer is zero or the question does not apply to you, enter 0.

39. What was your (and spouse's) adjusted gross income for 2000? Adjusted gross income is on IRS Form 1040–line 33; 1040A–line 19; 1040EZ–line 4; or Telefile–line I. $ ▢▢ , ▢▢▢

40. Enter the total amount of your (and spouse's) income tax for 2000. Income tax amount is on IRS Form 1040–line 51; 1040A–line 33; 1040EZ–line 10; or Telefile–line K. $ ▢▢ , ▢▢▢

41. Enter your (and spouse's) exemptions for 2000. Exemptions are on IRS Form 1040–line 6d or on Form 1040A–line 6d. For Form 1040EZ or Telefile, **see page 2.**

42-43. How much did you (and spouse) earn from working in 2000? Answer this question whether or not you filed a tax return. This information may be on your W-2 forms, or on IRS Form 1040–lines 7 + 12 + 18; 1040A–line 7; or 1040EZ–line 1. Telefilers should use their W-2's.

You (42) $ ▢▢ , ▢▢▢
Your Spouse (43) $ ▢▢ , ▢▢▢

Student (and Spouse) Worksheets (44-46)

44-46. Go to Page 8 and complete the columns on the left of Worksheets A, B, and C. Enter the student (and spouse) totals in questions 44, 45, and 46, respectively. Even though you may have few of the Worksheet items, check each line carefully.

Worksheet A (44) $ ▢▢ , ▢▢▢
Worksheet B (45) $ ▢▢ , ▢▢▢
Worksheet C (46) $ ▢▢ , ▢▢▢

47. As of today, what is the net worth of your (and spouse's) current **investments**? **See page 2.** $ ▢▢ , ▢▢▢

48. As of today, what is the net worth of your (and spouse's) current **businesses and/or investment farms**? **See page 2.** Do not include a farm that you live on and operate. $ ▢▢ , ▢▢▢

49. As of today, what is your (and spouse's) total current balance of cash, savings, and checking accounts? $ ▢▢ , ▢▢▢

50-51. If you receive veterans education benefits, for **how many months** from July 1, 2001 through June 30, 2002 will you receive these benefits, and **what amount** will you receive per month? Do not include your spouse's veterans education benefits.

Months (50) ▢▢
Amount (51) $ ▢▢▢

Step Three: Answer all seven questions in this step.

52. Were you born before January 1, 1978? ....   Yes ○ 1   No ○ 2

53. Will you be working on a master's or doctorate program (such as an MA, MBA, MD, JD, or Ph.D., etc.) during the school year 2001-2002? ....   Yes ○ 1   No ○ 2

54. As of today, are you married? (Answer "Yes" if you are separated but not divorced.) ....   Yes ○ 1   No ○ 2

55. Do you have children who receive more than half of their support from you? ....   Yes ○ 1   No ○ 2

56. Do you have dependents (other than your children or spouse) who live with you and who receive more than half of their support from you, now and through June 30, 2002? ....   Yes ○ 1   No ○ 2

57. Are you an orphan or ward of the court or were you a ward of the court until age 18? ....   Yes ○ 1   No ○ 2

58. Are you a veteran of the U.S. Armed Forces? **See page 2.** ....   Yes ○ 1   No ○ 2

If you (the student) answer "No" to every question in Step Three, go to Step Four.
If you answer "Yes" to any question in Step Three, skip Step Four and go to Step Five.

(If you are a graduate health profession student, your school may require you to complete Step Four even if you answered "Yes" in Step Three.)

Step Four: Complete this step if you (the student) answered "No" to all questions in Step Three.

59. Go to page 7 to determine who is considered a parent for this step. What is your parents' marital status as of today?

(Pick one.)   Married/Remarried ○ 1   Single ○ 2   Divorced/Separated ○ 3   Widowed ○ 4

60-63. What are your parents' Social Security Numbers and last names?
If your parent does not have a Social Security Number, enter 000-00-0000

60. FATHER'S/STEPFATHER'S SOCIAL SECURITY NUMBER   X X X – X X – X X X X

61. FATHER'S/STEPFATHER'S LAST NAME   F O R   I N F O R M A T I O N   O N L Y

62. MOTHER'S/STEPMOTHER'S SOCIAL SECURITY NUMBER   X X X – X X – X X X X

63. MOTHER'S/STEPMOTHER'S LAST NAME   D O   N O T   S U B M I T

64. Go to page 7 to determine how many people are in your parents' household.

65. Go to page 7 to determine how many in question 64 **(exclude your parents)** will be college students between July 1, 2001 and June 30, 2002.

66. What is your parents' state of legal residence?   STATE

67. Did your parents become legal residents of the state in question 66 before January 1, 1996?   Yes ○ 1   No ○ 2

68. If the answer to question 67 is "No," give the month and year legal residency began for the parent who has lived in the state the longest.   MONTH / YEAR

69. What is the age of your older parent?

70. For 2000, have your parents completed their IRS income tax return or another tax return listed in **question 71**?

a. My parents have already completed their return. ○ 1

b. My parents will file, but they have not yet completed their return. ○ 2

c. My parents are not going to file. **(Skip to question 76.)** ○ 3

71. What income tax return did your parents file or will they file for 2000?

a. IRS 1040 .... ○ 1

b. IRS 1040A, 1040EZ, 1040Telefile ..... ○ 2

c. A foreign tax return. See Page 2. ...... ○ 3

d. A tax return for Puerto Rico, Guam, American Samoa, the Virgin Islands, the Marshall Islands, the Federated States of Micronesia, or Palau. **See Page 2.** .... ○ 4

72. If your parents have filed or will file a 1040, were they eligible to file a 1040A or 1040EZ? **See page 2.**   Yes ○ 1   No ○ 2   Don't Know ○ 3

For questions 73 - 83, if the answer is zero or the question does not apply, enter 0.

73. What was your parents' adjusted gross income for 2000? Adjusted gross income is on IRS Form 1040–line 33; 1040A–line 19; 1040EZ–line 4; or Telefile–line I. $

74. Enter the total amount of your parents' income tax for 2000. Income tax amount is on IRS Form 1040–line 51; 1040A–line 33; 1040EZ–line 10; or Telefile–line K. $

75. Enter your parents' exemptions for 2000. Exemptions are on IRS Form 1040–line 6d or on Form 1040A–line 6d. For Form 1040EZ or Telefile, **see page 2.**

76-77. How much did your parents earn from working in 2000? Answer this question whether or not your parents filed a tax return. This information may be on their W-2 forms, or on IRS Form 1040–lines 7 + 12 + 18; 1040A–line 7; or 1040EZ–line 1. Telefilers should use their W-2's.

Father/Stepfather (76) $

Mother/Stepmother (77) $

Parent Worksheets (78-80)

78-80. Go to Page 8 and complete the columns on the right of Worksheets A, B, and C. Enter the parent totals in questions 78, 79, and 80, respectively. Even though your parents may have few of the Worksheet items, check each line carefully.

Worksheet A (78) $

Worksheet B (79) $

Worksheet C (80) $

81. As of today, what is the net worth of your parents' current **investments**? **See page 2.** $

82. As of today, what is the net worth of your parents' current **businesses and/or investment farms**? **See page 2.** Do not include a farm that your parents live on and operate. $

83. As of today, what is your parents' total current balance of cash, savings, and checking accounts? $

Now go to Step Six.

Step Five: Complete this step only if you (the student) answered "Yes" to any question in Step Three.

84. Go to **page 7** to determine how many people are in your (and your spouse's) household.

85. Go to **page 7** to determine how many in question 84 will be college students between July 1, 2001 and June 30, 2002.

Step Six: Please tell us which schools should receive your information.

For each school (up to six), please provide the federal school code and your housing plans. Look for the federal school codes on the Internet at **www.fafsa.ed.gov**, at your college financial aid office, at your public library, or by asking your high school guidance counselor. If you cannot get the federal school code, write in the complete name, address, city, and state of the college.

				HOUSING PLANS
86. 1ST FEDERAL SCHOOL CODE	OR	NAME OF COLLEGE / ADDRESS AND CITY	STATE	**87.** on campus 1 / off campus 2 / with parent 3
88. 2ND FEDERAL SCHOOL CODE	OR	NAME OF COLLEGE / ADDRESS AND CITY	STATE	**89.** on campus 1 / off campus 2 / with parent 3
90. 3RD FEDERAL SCHOOL CODE	OR	NAME OF COLLEGE / ADDRESS AND CITY	STATE	**91.** on campus 1 / off campus 2 / with parent 3
92. 4TH FEDERAL SCHOOL CODE	OR	NAME OF COLLEGE / ADDRESS AND CITY	STATE	**93.** on campus 1 / off campus 2 / with parent 3
94. 5TH FEDERAL SCHOOL CODE	OR	NAME OF COLLEGE / ADDRESS AND CITY	STATE	**95.** on campus 1 / off campus 2 / with parent 3
96. 6TH FEDERAL SCHOOL CODE	OR	NAME OF COLLEGE / ADDRESS AND CITY	STATE	**97.** on campus 1 / off campus 2 / with parent 3

Step Seven: Please read, sign, and date.

By signing this application, you agree, if asked, to provide information that will verify the accuracy of your completed form. This information may include your U.S. or state income tax forms. Also, you certify that you (1) will use federal and/or state student financial aid only to pay the cost of attending an institution of higher education, (2) are not in default on a federal student loan or have made satisfactory arrangements to repay it, (3) do not owe money back on a federal student grant or have made satisfactory arrangements to repay it, (4) will notify your school if you default on a federal student loan, and (5) understand that **the Secretary of Education has the authority to verify information reported on this application with the Internal Revenue Service.** If you purposely give false or misleading information, you may be fined $10,000, sent to prison, or both.

98. Date this form was completed.

MONTH / DAY / 2001 ○ or 2002 ○

99. Student signature (Sign in box)

FOR INFORMATION ONLY.

Parent signature (one parent whose information is provided in Step Four) (Sign in box)

DO NOT SUBMIT.

If this form was filled out by someone other than you, your spouse, or your parent(s), that person must complete this part.

Preparer's name, firm, and address

100. Preparer's Social Security Number (or 101)

101. Employer ID number (or 100)

102. Preparer's signature and date

SCHOOL USE ONLY: Federal School Code

D/O ○ 1

FAA SIGNATURE

MDE USE ONLY: Special Handle

Notes for questions 59–83 (page 5) Step Four: Who is considered a parent in this step?

Read these notes to determine who is considered a parent for purposes of this form. **Answer all questions in Step Four about them**, even if you do not live with them.

If your parents are both living and married to each other, answer the questions about them.

If your parent is widowed or single, answer the questions about that parent. If your widowed parent has remarried as of today, answer the questions about that parent **and** the person whom your parent married (your stepparent).

If your parents have divorced or separated, answer the questions about the parent you lived with more during the past 12 months. (If you did not live with one parent more than the other, give answers about the parent who provided more financial support during the last 12 months, or during the most recent year that you actually received support from a parent.) If this parent has remarried as of today, answer the questions on the rest of this form about that parent **and** the person whom your parent married (your stepparent).

Notes for question 64 (page 5)

Include in your parents' household (see notes, above, for who is considered a parent):
- your parents and yourself, even if you don't live with your parents, and
- your parents' other children if (a) your parents will provide more than half of their support from July 1, 2001 through June 30, 2002 or (b) the children could answer "No" to every question in Step Three, and
- other people if they now live with your parents, your parents provide more than half of their support, and your parents will continue to provide more than half of their support from July 1, 2001 through June 30, 2002.

Notes for questions 65 (page 5) and 85 (page 6)

Always count yourself as a college student. **Do not include your parents.** Include others only if they will attend at least half time in 2001-2002 a program that leads to a college degree or certificate.

Notes for question 84 (page 6)

Include in your (and your spouse's) household:
- yourself (and your spouse, if you have one), and
- your children, if you will provide more than half of their support from July 1, 2001 through June 30, 2002, and
- other people if they now live with you, and you provide more than half of their support, and you will continue to provide more than half of their support from July 1, 2001 through June 30, 2002.

Information on the Privacy Act and use of your Social Security Number

We use the information that you provide on this form to determine if you are eligible to receive federal student financial aid and the amount that you are eligible to receive. Section 483 of the Higher Education Act of 1965, as amended, gives us the authority to ask you and your parents these questions, and to collect the Social Security Numbers of you and your parents.

State and institutional student financial aid programs may also use the information that you provide on this form to determine if you are eligible to receive state and institutional aid and the need that you have for such aid. Therefore, we will disclose the information that you provide on this form to each institution you list in questions 86–97, state agencies in your state of legal residence, and the state agencies of the states in which the colleges that you list in questions 86–97 are located.

If you are applying solely for federal aid, you must answer all of the following questions that apply to you: 1–9, 13–15, 24, 27–28, 31–32, 35, 36–40, 42–49, 52–66, 69–74, 76–85, and 98–99. If you do not answer these questions, you will not receive federal aid.

Without your consent, we may disclose information that you provide to entities under a published "routine use." Under such a routine use, we may disclose information to third parties that we have authorized to assist us in administering the above programs; to other federal agencies under computer matching programs, such as those with the Internal Revenue Service, Social Security Administration, Selective Service System, Immigration and Naturalization Service, and Veterans Administration; to your parents or spouse; and to members of Congress if you ask them to help you with student aid questions.

If the federal government, the U.S. Department of Education, or an employee of the U.S. Department of Education is involved in litigation, we may send information to the Department of Justice, or a court or adjudicative body, if the disclosure is related to financial aid and certain conditions are met. In addition, we may send your information to a foreign, federal, state, or local enforcement agency if the information that you submitted indicates a violation or potential violation of law, for which that agency has jurisdiction for investigation or prosecution. Finally, we may send information regarding a claim that is determined to be valid and overdue to a consumer reporting agency. This information includes identifiers from the record; the amount, status, and history of the claim; and the program under which the claim arose.

State Certification

By submitting this application, you are giving your state financial aid agency permission to verify any statement on this form and to obtain income tax information for all persons required to report income on this form.

The Paperwork Reduction Act of 1995

The Paperwork Reduction Act of 1995 says that no one is required to respond to a collection of information unless it displays a valid OMB control number, which for this form is 1845-0001. The time required to complete this form is estimated to be one hour, including time to review instructions, search data resources, gather the data needed, and complete and review the information collection. If you have comments about this estimate or suggestions for improving this form, please write to: U.S. Department of Education, Washington DC 20202-4651.

We may request additional information from you to ensure efficient application processing operations. We will collect this additional information only as needed and on a voluntary basis.

Worksheets

Do not mail these worksheets in with your application.
Keep these worksheets; your school may ask to see them.

Worksheet A
Calendar Year 2000

For question 44 Student/Spouse		For question 78 Parent(s)
$	Earned income credit from IRS Form 1040–line 60a; 1040A–line 38a; 1040EZ–line 8a; or Telefile–line L	$
$	Additional child tax credit from IRS Form 1040–line 62 or 1040A–line 39	$
$	Welfare benefits, including Temporary Assistance for Needy Families (TANF). Don't include food stamps.	$
$	Social Security benefits received that were not taxed (such as SSI)	$
$ — Enter in question 44.		Enter in question 78. — $

Worksheet B
Calendar Year 2000

For question 45 Student/Spouse		For question 79 Parent(s)
$	Payments to tax-deferred pension and savings plans (paid directly or withheld from earnings), including amounts reported on the W-2 Form in Box 13, codes D, E, F, G, H, and S	$
$	IRA deductions and payments to self-employed SEP, SIMPLE, and Keogh and other qualified plans from IRS Form 1040–total of lines 23 + 29 or 1040A–line 16	$
$	Child support **received** for all children. Don't include foster care or adoption payments.	$
$	Tax exempt interest income from IRS Form 1040–line 8b or 1040A–line 8b	$
$	Foreign income exclusion from IRS Form 2555–line 43 or 2555EZ–line 18	$
$	Untaxed portions of pensions from IRS Form 1040–lines (15a minus 15b) + (16a minus 16b) or 1040A–lines (11a minus 11b) + (12a minus 12b) excluding rollovers	$
$	Credit for federal tax on special fuels from IRS Form 4136–line 9 – nonfarmers only	$
$	Housing, food, and other living allowances paid to members of the military, clergy, and others (including cash payments and cash value of benefits)	$
$	Veterans noneducation benefits such as Disability, Death Pension, or Dependency & Indemnity Compensation (DIC) and/or VA Educational Work-Study allowances	$
$	Any other untaxed income or benefits not reported elsewhere on Worksheets A and B, such as worker's compensation, untaxed portions of railroad retirement benefits, Black Lung Benefits, Refugee Assistance, etc. **Don't include** student aid, Workforce Investment Act educational benefits, or benefits from flexible spending arrangements, e.g., cafeteria plans.	$
$	Cash **received**, or any money paid on your behalf, not reported elsewhere on this form	XXXXXXXX
$ — Enter in question 45.		Enter in question 79. — $

Worksheet C
Calendar Year 2000

For question 46 Student/Spouse		For question 80 Parent(s)
$	Education credits (Hope and Lifetime Learning tax credits) from IRS Form 1040-line 46 or 1040A–line 29	$
$	Child support **paid** because of divorce or separation. Do not include support for children in your (or your parents') household, as reported in question 84 (or question 64 for your parents).	$
$	Taxable earnings from Federal Work-Study or other need-based work programs	$
$	Student grant, scholarship, and fellowship aid, including AmeriCorps awards, that was reported to the IRS in your (or your parents') adjusted gross income	$
$ — Enter in question 46.		Enter in question 80. — $